House Beautiful

ELEMENTS OF style

THE EDITORS OF House Beautiful MAGAZINE

TEXT BY Christine Pittel

HEARST BOOKS

A Division of Sterling Publishing Co., Inc.

NEW YORK

This book was previously published as a hardcover under the title *House Beautiful Great Style*.

PRODUCED BY SMALLWOOD & STEWART, INC., NEW YORK
Editor: Rachel Carley
Designer: Susi Oberhelman

Library of Congress Cataloging-in-Publication Data
Available upon request.

10 9 8 7 6 5 4 3 2 1

First Paperback Edition 2003
Published by Hearst Books
A Division of Sterling Publishing Company, Inc.
387 Park Avenue South, New York, NY 10016

House Beautiful and Hearst Books are trademarks owned by
Hearst Magazines Property, Inc., in USA, and Hearst Communications, Inc., in Canada.

www.housebeautiful.com

Distributed in Canada by Sterling Publishing
c/o Canadian Manda Group, One Atlantic Avenue, Suite 105
Toronto, Ontario, Canada M6K 3E7

Distributed in Australia by Capricorn Link (Australia) Pty. Ltd.
P.O. Box 704, Windsor, NSW 2756 Australia

Printed in Singapore

ISBN 1-58816-315-6

HOUSE BEAUTIFUL DEDICATES THIS

BOOK TO THE MEMORY OF BETTY BOOTE,

THE MAGAZINE'S MANAGING EDITOR

FOR SIXTEEN YEARS, WITH AFFECTION

AND RESPECT AND GRATITUDE.

contents

ANNUAL GARDENING NUMBER

HOMES AND GARDENS OF CORNISH. ART OF GARDENING. SUBURBAN HOME AND
GARDEN. OUT-DOOR DINING ROOM. SUN-DIALS. FLOWERS FOR THE TABLE

PRICE 20 CENTS   MARCH $2.00 A YEAR

THE HOUSE BEAUTIFUL

L·KENNEDY·

PUBLISHED MONTHLY BY

THE HOUSE BEAUTIFUL COMPANY

REPUBLIC BUILDING, CHICAGO

foreword

Vol. 1. No. 1. DECEMBER, 1896. PRICE, 10 CENTS.

THE HOUSE
BEAUTIFUL

WEST HAVES
EAST BEST

A·MONTHLY·MAGAZINE··OF
ART·AND·ARTISANSHIP

WHEN WE BEGAN PLANNING HOUSE BEAUTIFUL'S 1996 Centennial celebration, we knew we wanted to publish a book that captured the stylistic essence of the magazine that was the first in America to be dedicated to the home. A look back at all the issues produced over our hundred-year history confirmed my feeling that style is essentially about people, the special creative people who give each decade its particular look. And so we are opening this book with a backward glance at those who led the way in the decoration of houses. They are familiar names — Elsie de Wolfe, Frank Lloyd Wright, Van Day Truex, Billy Baldwin, T. H. Robsjohn-Gibbings, Sister Parish — and with each name a special vision comes to mind. From there we move to the stylemakers of today, decorators like John Saladino, Victoria Hagan, and Mariette Himes Gomez in New York; Jacques Grange, Christian Liaigre, and Frédéric Méchiche in Paris; Nancy Braithwaite in Atlanta; Barbara Barry in Los Angeles; Nancy Kitchell in Scottsdale. Look at their work and you will see that each has a clear vision, a distinct point of view.

To give voice to those visions, we asked Christine Pittel, a gifted writer and contributing editor of *House Beautiful*, to develop a text that would capture all the subtle elements of style and of design philosophy.

Any book, like any magazine, is the work of many people. We want to acknowledge the enormous contribution of the designers whose work is shown here, the generosity of their clients, the artistry of the photographers who captured their combined visions, and the many *House Beautiful* editors who produced the stories that are included in these pages. As you peruse them, remember the wise words of the distinguished designer Albert Hadley, who reminds us that "Decoration is not some mystery. It's the expression of personality."

For one hundred years, House Beautiful has been reporting on those myriad "expressions of personality." As we move into our second century, the whole nation seems to be rededicating itself to the home, to all that goes into it, to all that it gives back. And we will be right there to help and to inspire.

The Editors
HOUSE BEAUTIFUL

introduction

blithely whited out Victorian gloom. Jean-Michel Frank papered the walls with ivory parchment. Frank Lloyd Wright stretched and spun and broke open the box until a house fused into the landscape. Charles and Ray Eames erected a steel-and-glass home from industrial parts and furnished it with molded plywood chairs. Sister Parish piled on cheerful chintz and needle-point cushions and Pekingese pups.

For one hundred years, *House Beautiful* has been a showcase for that alluring attribute called style. When the magazine debuted in 1896, it was the first ever to be devoted to the home. It opened the front door and introduced readers to the people, places, and per-ceptions that set new directions in the course of architecture and design.

But style doesn't preclude sub-stance. From the very first issue, *House Beautiful* took a definite point of view. Dismissing the typical Victorian house as a "hideous aggregation" of "dismal dreariness" and "tawdry finery," the magazine discovered a more enduring beauty in simplicity. Rather than feature

Born in 1865, Elsie de Wolfe was America's first and most famous professional female decorator. An early stint in the theater was more memorable for the back flip she did on stage than for any acting ability, so through sheer force of personality she invented a new career. ■ De Wolfe swept out Victorian clutter, painted ponderous mahogany furniture white, moved trellis indoors, and made chintz chic; a single pattern enlightens a New York bedroom shown in 1913 (above). ■ At sixty, the designer married a British diplomat, Sir Charles Mendl. Lady Mendl, dressed in Mainbocher (opposite), was painted by Cecil Beaton in the 1930s.

ersatz copies of elaborate Louis XIV *fauteuils*, the editors preferred the more modest virtues of "direct, graceful, simple and refined" American Colonial furniture, and vowed "to urge the truth of the maxim that whatever is useful is beautiful." While others were slavishly imitating European manors, *House Beautiful* championed the brave new architecture of America's homegrown genius, Frank Lloyd Wright.

Wright's own Oak Park, Illinois, house was published in the third issue, beginning a long association with the magazine that culminated in several

In a 1930 penthouse (top), Gilbert Rohde combined black linoleum, leather, lacquer, and chrome in the Streamline Moderne style, inspired by images of speed and fluidity associated with a new transportation age. ■ Jean-Michel Frank's 1928 drawing room for the Vicomte de Noailles — photographed by Man Ray (above left) — made the designer famous; lined in parchment, the room had white bronze doors and furniture veneered in straw. ■ In a 1936 pared-down Paris apartment (above right), the great French Modernist left the walls and floor bare.

special issues devoted to Wright alone. His vision dovetailed with the Arts and Crafts aesthetic that dominated design horizons through World War I. In the 1920s, the Arts and Crafts movement gave way to an exuberant eclectic revivalism, soon challenged by the various strains of Modernism: Art Deco, Bauhaus, International Style, and Streamline Moderne. As early as 1928, *House Beautiful* published the exquisitely sleek and simple rooms of French Modernist Jean-Michel Frank, whose influence on other designers has grown even stronger with time.

In his sixteenth-century Tudor cottage in Kent, England, published in a 1935 issue, Noel Coward papered the walls of his barroom with pages from scripts, but wisely left the half-timbered bedroom alone (top). ■ Four years later, architect Richard Neutra won the magazine's Small House Competition with an International Style design (above left), featuring ribbon windows and crisp white planes. Modernism promised to deliver space and light to the masses with an open floor plan (above right), used here by Bauhaus architects Walter Gropius and Marcel Breuer.

House Beautiful not only reflected the taste of each era, but often helped shape it as well. As the country was recovering from the depths of the Depression and wartime austerity, it published the work of New York decorator Dorothy Draper, who liked a touch of drama with her damask and declared, "The Drab Age is over. Color is coming into its own again." After World War II, the magazine promoted the one-story ranch-style house — preferably oriented around a private patio protected from cars whizzing by — as appropriate to family life in the suburbs. Throughout the 1950s, the featured Pace Setter houses exemplified the latest ideas in climate control and labor-saving devices, perpetuating *House Beautiful's* long-standing practical streak. For decades, the editors published fold-out blueprints and detailed specs so potential home builders could benefit from the services of an architect and obtain a good design for the price of a magazine.

Yet running parallel to this egalitarian, democratic attitude applauding

Overscaled red cabbage roses, dark greens, and chalk-white neo-Baroque plasterwork were Dorothy Draper's trademarks, used to big, bold effect in a 1943 living room converted from a garage to ease the wartime housing shortage (above left). ■ Ancient Greece, Scandinavian Modern furniture, and such basic forms as the sawbuck table were inspirations for T. H. Robsjohn-Gibbings (top), who designed this dining room suite in 1950 (center left). ■ In a double-height living room finished in glass and steel, Charles and Ray Eames floated a painting for the pleasure of anyone leaning back on their Eames chair and ottoman (center right). ■ A 1955 issue (above right) was devoted to American architecture's "everflowing fountainhead, Frank Lloyd Wright."

accessible, commonsense elegance was a healthy curiosity about the rich and famous, and an undeniable fascination with glamour. Jacqueline Kennedy Onassis's Fifth Avenue apartment was published for the first and only time in *House Beautiful*, when she offered it as a backdrop to promote a favorite charity. *House Beautiful* walked readers through Cecil Beaton's romantic rose-bowered eighteenth-century English country estate and quoted Elizabeth, the Queen Mother, who confided on a visit, "How clever of you, Sir Cecil, to have made everything look so shabby!"

Personalities also reigned in the decorating world. Dorothy May (Sister) Parish, who was born to pearls, delighted in wearing pop beads. Like the best American institutions, there was no bunk about this redoubtable designer, who ruled for six decades until her death at age 84 in 1994. Merely by collecting more than a few of her favorite things, she could make a just-bought penthouse look like old money. Legendary American decorator Billy Baldwin was a Southern gentleman of

Concrete block became poetic in Wright's magisterial, Mayan-style Ennis house (above left) overlooking Los Angeles. ■ *House Beautiful's* Pace Setter houses broke new ground and shook up conventions. A 1959 model (center) was oriented around an enclosed swimming-pool court topped by a screened space-frame. ■ The magazine recognized that style is not solely the province of decorators. Artist Georgia O'Keeffe (top) respected the elemental nature of her century-old adobe house in Abiquiu, New Mexico, featured in *House Beautiful* in 1963. Beyond her weathered wood doors under a hand-hewn beam (above right) was an ever-changing still life of light and shadow, pared down to the sun-bleached bone.

the old school who brought a new clarity to traditional style. He was famous for dark walls—lacquered brown leather in Cole Porter's library and, in his own 1946 living room, the glossy green of a wet gardenia leaf. He wanted nothing to do with fuss and could make tailored cotton look as sumptuous as silk. "Some people confuse luxury with grandeur," Baldwin once said. "To me, comfort is perhaps the ultimate luxury."

As styles constantly shifted—the biomorphic 1950s led into Pop and Op Art in the 1960s and a profusion of

Understated luxury was Billy Baldwin's specialty, as in a poolside loggia in Mallorca (top), shown in a 1969 issue. Unpretentious wicker furniture is arranged with clarity and cohesion around a simple Parsons table. ■ English decorator David Hicks composed unexpected tablescapes of pure white objects in his wife Lady Pamela Mountbatten's study (above left); the grisaille murals by Rex Whistler were inherited. ■ Style-setter Nancy Lancaster came from a fine old Virginia family with a habit of marrying into the British aristocracy, and she knew great houses from the inside out. She owned the decorating firm of Colefax & Fowler, and livened up the faded English country house look with a vibrant elegance and ease, evident in her library (above right).

pattern on pattern—there were always those who sought refuge in classicism and the timeless beauty of the past. But the innovators were smart enough to make reference to antiquity, then reinterpret the elements in a fresh way. The candy-coated post-Modernism of the 1970s, which drew strength from the historic preservation movement, represented classicism with a twist.

Design seems to run in cycles, as the pendulum swings back and forth between opulence and simplicity. The extravagant 1980s sparked the opposite reaction in the 1990s, as people attempt to pare down. Then there are the renegades, those self-confident souls who like to throw everything up in the air and see what comes down. *House Beautiful* has always encouraged new thinking. In 1929, it published Buckminster Fuller's utopian Dymaxion

Some of the most memorable rooms may never have seen a decorator's swatch, but they shine because the personality of the owner comes through. ■ In Truman Capote's Long Island house (above left), featured in 1969, a blue-painted floor recalling the sea was lacquered to a mirror finish. The small chaise in front of the fireplace belonged to his dog, and the hats come from his sizable collection. ■ Sister Parish, the grande dame of the decorating profession (top), also created rooms that looked personal, as if imbued with the memories of generations. ■ Her own Manhattan living room, shown in the late 1960s (above right), was a compendium of cherished objects and comfortable furniture set against stylish glossy brown walls.

House, a radical six-sided habitat suspended from a mast. Even Nelson Rockefeller broke out of stereotype with his 1978 Japanese-style home in Pocantico Hills, which embodied the Eastern ideals of serenity and repose. Rockefeller's desire to return to simplicity was no surprise to *House Beautiful* readers, who had already digested a whole issue devoted to the Japanese concept of shibui—the art of restraint and nuance. Some could even discern an underlying relationship between traditional Japanese design and Modernism, as practiced, for example, by Richard Meier. The architect's cleanlined, disciplined 1978 house on Long

Van Day Truex inspired a generation of students as president of Parsons School of Design. Simple rattan chairs covered in natural wool and hemp carpets in closely related tones created a sense of tranquility in his French farmhouse (top). ■ Jacqueline Kennedy Onassis showed off fabrics from Bedford Stuyvesant's Design Works in her dining room (above left), shown in 1971. ■ Who cared if the "Japanese" conservatory (center) on Cecil Beaton's Wiltshire estate had Gothic windows? Certainly not Sir Cecil (above right), whose house was also featured in the 1970s.

Island, an abstraction of points and planes, shares purities of structure with Japanese design. In fact, both could be described with the same words, meant as high praise in the first issue: "direct, graceful, simple and refined."

Although the vision changes, the words remain the same. In 1946, the editors decreed, "The new ostentation will be unostentation." The statement still resonates today. Simplicity is once again a virtue. After one hundred years, the magazine seems to have come right back to where it started. People are once again reassessing values. Period rooms are a thing of the past. Designers are more inclined to mix than match, and their unexpected juxtapositions capture the energy of a compellingly diverse present. Rather than one mode, there are many. With an almost infinite variety of rooms in the following pages, *House Beautiful* celebrates a century of great style — and the start of another.

Japanese craftsmen spent two years building a composition of rare woods and sliding partitions for Nelson Rockefeller (above left). "We have taken the essence of the historic Japanese style and brought it up to contemporary form," explained Rockefeller, who commissioned master woodworker George Nakashima to design the furniture. ▤ A 1978 house on Long Island designed by architect Richard Meier (above right) was a cool collage of color and space, maintaining the Modernist passion for form revealed by light. "Bold color accentuates certain planes and depresses others," says Meier.

THE stylemakers

CERTAIN PEOPLE CAN TAKE A CHICKEN COOP AND MAKE IT
stunning. For them, design has no boundaries. They are always
pushing the envelope — making that chartreuse paint a little
more citric, hanging coarse burlap instead of fine silk at a
window, removing every picture from a room but one.

THESE ARE THE STYLEMAKERS. THEIR WORK NOT ONLY
invigorates their clients, but also influences other designers,
subtly shifting and shaping the look of an era. Some are formally
trained, others self-taught. All are exceptionally intuitive. They
seem to sense just what a room needs, often before anyone else
is even aware that something is missing. They can confront the
most familiar scenario — a dining table and six chairs, a sofa
and a fireplace — and come up with a fresh approach.

RELYING ON TALENT AND WITS RATHER THAN RULE, EACH
of these great designers has his or her own approach. John
Saladino, responsible for this resplendent dining room, likes to
conjure antiquity out of thin air. Others create rooms that look
as unaffected as a primitive pine table. For all their individuality, however, they share a common bond: a vision of what life in
a well-appointed house should be like.

JOHN
saladino

The lush, soaring plaint of a Puccini aria seems to linger in the air. John Saladino designs rooms with a past. In an era of nonchalance, when others take refuge in neutrality, he is not afraid of emotion and grandeur. Steeped in history, sensuous to the touch, and brushed with extraordinary colors — like the haunting mauve of the evening sky just before nightfall — his dramatic compositions seem to capture and imply age and boundless time. The ultimate effect is otherworldly, and yet completely of the moment. Saladino is a modernist in his approach to space and light, who happens to speak with a classical vocabulary. "I make my own reality," he says with a Delphic smile.

His compelling interiors are achieved by manipulating a few key components. "I work with three scales in every room — monumental, residential, and human," he says. Monumental refers to the architecture (this is a man well acquainted with coffered ceilings and tapestries sized for a castle). Residential scale comes from the rooms within rooms created with furniture arrangements. Human scale involves such apparently incidental issues as the length of a breakfast table. (For intimacy, the designer prefers a span of no more than seven feet between diners.)

As deftly as Saladino juggles scale, he conjures color. He has the maestro's gift of perfect pitch, with pigment. His palette is one of the most unusual in the design world. Strange, icy blues are apt to segue from

John Saladino is the master of magnificent amber-tinted decay, and not above dumping coffee into a wheelbarrow of plaster to create instant antiquity. In this 1920s California hacienda, he sandblasted white paint off the stone walls and stripped the beams, but not perfectly, so traces would remain. "The point of aging is to let some of those wrinkles show," he says. ■ An 11-foot Piranesi etching establishes a monumental scale in the living room (opposite), in contrast to the human scale set by Saladino's Balustrade table. ■ The transluscent glass of a compote plays off the solidity of the dining table (above), crowned with a circle of flame-scorched marble. ■ Saladino relishes surprises, like using his signature quilted cotton slipcovers on an eighteenth-century chair or setting an ornately carved Portuguese mirror on a chenille tapestry (overleaf).

platinum to periwinkle to amethyst; then, unexpectedly, he might fling a few molten, magenta-colored cushions on a Renaissance chair. "Magenta is a glorious color in caviar amounts," says Saladino, who loves the red range, starting with pale, dusty powder pink and moving through raspberry to coral. Iridescent silks, the kind that look blue from one direction and red from another, fascinate him. Flouting conventional wisdom, he puts the lightest fabrics nearest the windows and the darkest in the shadows. He loves elusive, metamorphic colors that change with the time of day. "If you're going to do black, don't do *black*," he remarks. "Do something rich and dark that you'll perceive as black at night, but in the daytime might be midnight blue or the color of espresso coffee."

For Saladino, pattern is the quickest way to violate the serenity of a room. He always upholsters the sofa in a solid color to blend into the carpet or walls so it will "disappear." But that doesn't mean pattern is banished. He simply reserves the shimmering gold-dusted Fortuny velvets he favors to cover a pillow or drape over a table.

Like a great couturier, Saladino is constantly copied, but nobody designs with his bravura. He's interested in space as an emotional experience. "A beautiful room," says the designer, "can be a moment of transcendence."

Saladino rooms are a radiant mélange of old and new. "History for me," he says, "is a living source of nourishment." ■ In the master suite, a contemporary wall of gridded glass separates bedroom and bath. The bathroom sink (above) is hollowed out from a single piece of stone. ■ Saladino designed the comfortable sofa at the foot of the seventeenth-century Italian bed (opposite) and mounted the mirror on two lengths of hemp. With this designer, worn oriental rugs gain new status; Saladino loves the soft patina of the warp threads showing through. The white paint was left on the stone walls because the owners of the house like to wake up in a bright room.

VICTORIA
hagan

LIKE ONE OF DOROTHY PARKER'S BONS MOTS, A Victoria Hagan room feels spontaneous, unexpected, and succinctly apt. Against a typical background of cool, pale walls with filmy white chiffon curtains billowing at the window—accentuating the buoyant sense of space and air and light—the New York designer sets out unusual objects in a spare, suggestive array. The wit lies in the way she juxtaposes disparate elements. Just what does a gaunt and tattered high-backed Jacobean chair say to a streamlined black leather-and-chrome seat by Mies van der Rohe? For a scintillating cocktail party, be sure to invite an assortment of guests.

Hagan's serene, sophisticated still lifes have made her one of the brightest stars in Manhattan's design firmament.

Her interiors feel utterly contemporary, yet with an aura of other worlds, other eras. "When I was studying art history, I was fascinated by the hidden meanings in paintings and the symbolism behind things," she recalls. She likes to think her rooms speak to people and tell a story in the same way.

What Hagan looks for in a piece of furniture is personality. All periods are equal. The same room might hold a late-Renaissance Aubusson tapestry, a 1950s glass coffee table, and an eighteenth-century wing chair. Propinquity brings out the relationships and contrasts among various styles. "I'm always playing with time," she says. She doesn't like to feel she's bound by rules, but there is a method. "I'm trying to find a rhythm between everything and achieve a balance," says Hagan. Her palette is both classic and quirky, just

Opposites attract. ■ The white floor and walls in the study of Hagan's Manhattan apartment (opposite), shared with her husband, set off black and white chairs posed like sculptures and connected by a stenciled zebra rug. Next to Mies van der Rohe's trim Brno design, an eighteenth-century Jacobean armchair exuding stuffing looks like someone's dissolute uncle. Hagan finds its lines inspirational and can't bear to reupholster it, explaining, "the soul of that chair is right there." ■ An Art Deco folding table (above) holds a typically eclectic mix: a plaster relief, a Mexican pitcher, leatherbound books, and an Italian candlestick made into a lamp.

like her antiques. She is apt to paint the walls subtle variations on white, then throw in an accessory in an off-color such as teal or chartreuse — as surprising as the first suck on a sour-ball. She loves the shimmer of Fortuny fabrics draped casually over a sofa. Nothing is ever stiff. She uses velvet the way someone else might use canvas, and treats canvas as if it were velvet.

Hagan's four years at New York's Parsons School of Design rooted her flights of fancy in fact. She likes the concept of minimalist interiors, but feels they can be uncomfortable. "Besides, I'm too much of a collector to be a minimalist," she admits. As a child, she hunted for treasures in the woods, digging up bits of old china and glass from what turned out to be the former town dump and fitting them back together. If she hadn't been a designer, she would have been an archaeologist.

"I'm still finding treasures, discovering something from the past and trying to make it beautiful and current," says Hagan. There's something elusive and enigmatic about her rooms, with the occasional gleam of silver in the shadows or a crystalline star on a table, refracting the light. She gives a room soul.

The icy palette of Hagan's dining room — the walls are painted her favorite shade of white (Pratt & Lambert Snowflake) — is spiked with the chartreuse of the beaded chandelier shades and the teal green of vinyl chairs from the 1940s. The nailheads, says Hagan, are worth every penny. "They define the lines of a piece and give a nice detail." ▪ A white linen tablecloth, custom-made with inverted corner pleats, has the casual elegance of a dropcloth (above). The designer loves the series of simply framed photographs depicting the oceans of the world because they all look the same, only different. ▪ An American Empire sofa (opposite), which was in Hagan's first showhouse room, is upholstered in white textured cotton. The candlesticks and compote are Venetian glass.

Transparencies and reflections frequently bring a sense of mystery to Hagan's interiors, as illustrated by the living room, where a ceiling painted silver gray between white beams helps reflect light. ▮ Propping a slender mirror on an Empire table enhances the effect (above). ▮ Diaphanous curtains of white chiffon (right) incandesce in the sun. The intaglios glued to the mantel are one of Hagan's alluring signature details.

WILLIAM
hodgins

On a whirlwind trip to Italy as a student at Parsons School of Design, William Hodgins was bewitched by Andrea Palladio and never looked back. The noble gravity and serene grandeur of the Renaissance architect's centuries-old villas drowsing on the hills and plains of the Veneto remained with him when he returned to New York City, and later in the more genteel milieu of Boston, where he moved in 1969 to start his own firm. Hodgins took the classical principles of Renaissance architecture, rooted in a certain harmony of form, scale, and proportion, to heart. As he explains it, "classical design feels strong and romantic at the same time, and that's very appealing."

In Hodgins' hands, the restraint and order inherent to classical design becomes breathtakingly contemporary in light and airy spaces touched by the sublime. If a room has no distinctive architectural elements, he will add them where appropriate, designing moldings or reconfiguring doorways to arrive at his ideal vision for the space.

Then he will probably paint every wall white. (Of the twelve different paint colors he may use in a single job, eleven will be shades of white.) He deliberately hushes the periphery of a room to better appreciate the gracefully arched back of a low-slung English

William Hodgins designs by harmony rather than dissonance, so his rooms speak for themselves with a whisper, not a shout. ▮ His own master bedroom in a handsome townhouse in Boston's Back Bay is a sea of tranquility (opposite). The mirror mounted above the fireplace of French limestone is made of marbleized bollection molding; the oval profile reflects a shape found in classical design. ▮ Hodgins appreciates the richness of detail illustrated by an inlaid Anglo-Indian table (above) and the arms of a late eighteenth-century Directoire chair, carved as winged maidens. ▮ The fearless designer put an overscaled garden statue and a working desk in the living room (overleaf). "I think it's strange that people go into a tiny little corner to do their work," says Hodgins. "Generally, I put my desk in the nicest, biggest room where the sunshine streams in. I like to work in the room where I like to live." The room also displays an ever-expanding collection of globes, astrolabes, and armillary spheres.

Regency chair or the more proper posture exhibited by its staunch and straight-armed French Empire cousin. The antique furniture (usually painted white as well) is arranged in conversational groupings. "I tend to pay particular attention to placement," he says. When growing up in Canada, he moved the furniture around constantly. "It drove my mother crazy," Hodgins says. "She never knew where things were going to be when she came home from work."

Hodgins gravitates toward the blur of old gilt, rubbed nearly bare by innumerable hands. Others might be lured by the lissome lines of a Louis XVI bergère, but Hodgins is more likely seduced by the flaking paint. Not at all fazed by a time-ravaged finish, he favors well-worn painted country furniture from Sweden and Denmark. He also loves the powdery, pitted surfaces of crumbling garden statues, eroding obelisks, and weather-beaten urns veiled in rust. He was among the first to bring garden ornaments indoors. "I like that crudeness," he explains. "Since I don't use a lot of pattern in my work, texture is very important; it softens a room." He likes mellow leathers and stone, a material that possesses that eternal quality he is always seeking

"One thinks of decorating as embellishment, but I'm always trying to keep everything as simple as possible," says Hodgins. "I aim for clarity and a sort of gentle dignity." His thoughtful, composed rooms are complete, but not cluttered. Like any good classic, they look as if they will last a long time.

Glints of gold amid the ivory and alabaster include a gilded bronze horse and snail from Peru, set on an oval mirrored *surtout* (above left). ■ The quintessential Hodgins chair combines graceful curves and a chipped and flaking painted finish (above right). ■ The dining room windows (opposite) appear as if dressed for a waltz, wearing pale celadon silk taffeta hanging from a tole valance. "I keep dragging those curtains from place to place," says Hodgins. Used as a dining banquette, the circa 1860 settee was soaked with rain when he picked it up along a Maine roadside. He had it recovered and painted the mahogany frame.

BARBARA barry

THINK OF HOLLYWOOD FILM NOIR IN THE 1940S, WITH a hard-boiled detective waiting in an unfamiliar living room for the blonde femme fatale to walk in the door and ruin his life. Los Angeles designer Barbara Barry understands that sort of glamour, particularly the cool, languid chic synonymous with southern California. Mix in the sleek Modernism of Jean-Michel Frank, the influential French designer known for his stark, creamy sofas and chunky club chairs, and the result is a sophisticated cocktail of memory and desire.

Barry's sepia-toned palette underlines the mood by creating the effect of a black-and-white movie set, translated into her personal color spectrum. "For me, there are only five colors in the world: sage green, mustard, taupe, oxblood, and dark chocolate brown," she says. "Green is my neutral. I even dream in green."

When Barry was a child her mother gave her an easel and pinned up her drawings. Although she grew up with confidence and a sure hand, she has no formal design training and never sought work in an established firm to see how things were supposed to be done. "I just make it up as I go along," says Barry, who starts designing a room by drawing it. "I sketch and then I see a line and I follow it and the line turns into something."

Barry finds her forms and then builds them into a balanced composition. The furniture is usually custom-designed in clean shapes inspired by Frank. "I think tailored; I think crisp," she declares. Dressmaking details like the box pleats on a sofa skirt, dark-green welting on a

French moderne meets California casual in this Los Angeles house decorated by Barbara Barry for a discriminating couple who "owned things that mean something to them and didn't want anything more." Barry added just enough to point up her clients' own furnishings. ■ The Le Corbusier table in the dining room (opposite) was a treasured possession; Barry designed upholstered chairs with waxed oak legs to counterbalance the floating glass top. The lamp shade of painted Fortuny silk was her response to the Islamic decoration of the ceiling, and provides the only bit of pattern in the room. Glinting silver candlesticks (above) are like "pieces of jewelry" completing the ensemble.

mustard pillow, or an oval button perfectly placed just above center on a chair back identify her signature pieces.

This attention to form and detail reflects Barry's ability to extend her reach beyond the surface. "I don't think of decoration as lamination, but as integration," she maintains. In designing a room, she tries to capture a certain sense of lifestyle. Her own era is the forties: "I love pageboys, cashmere twin sets, and pearls." That was also a time when Los Angeles was a magical oasis, with movie stars sipping martinis in the aqua light of the pool.

But Barry is not suggesting her clients live in a time warp; she's talking about the way people treat themselves. She believes that home should feel at least as luxurious as a fine hotel, with pressed linen sheets, thick towels, and the best shower head. She will stock a breakfast tray with a silver toast rack and line closets with wallpaper. "Life is about small moments, and I try to take my clients back to a place that was a little sweeter and a little more romantic than where we are now," she says.

The African masks and framed art in the entry (above) belonged to the owners of the house. Barry added the tansu chest from Japan and the mercury glass lamp from the 1940s, an era she loves for its movie-star glamour. ▪ Her signature palette of sepia tones distinguishes the handsome living room (opposite), where Barry painted the white doors a deep chocolate brown, and imbues the whole house with a retro flavor. The cubic club chair is Barry's homage to French Modernist Jean-Michel Frank. Massive and inviting, with a low center of gravity, it contributes to a dominant horizontality in the room that conveys a sense of tranquility. A low horizon line was a hallmark of Modernism.

Barry's rooms not only gain depth from layers of earthy color, but also from alliteration of form. ■ In the living room, she designed the rounded mahogany coffee table (left) to pick up the shapes in the Donald Sultan painting above the couch, then arranged the furniture around it in another circle, bound by a wool sisal rug. Sliding doors were replaced with more elegant hinged glass doors, which still keep the house open to the garden. ■ The end table (above) is another Barry design, made of white oak that has been bleached, wire-brushed, rubbed with white paint, sanded, and finally waxed.

BUNNY williams

BUNNY WILLIAMS DESIGNS THE KIND OF RELAXED, comfortable rooms where people head straight for the plumpest sofa, put their feet up, and settle in to read the newspaper. "I think that's why people come to me," she says. "A house is not for show. It's to be lived in."

First the New York designer quizzes her clients on their habits. Do they watch TV or play cards? Covet fine antiques or favor sturdy country pieces that stand up to children? Prefer a formal dining room or a casual eat-in kitchen? "Tell me what makes your heart sing," says Williams to her clients. "We'll start with the basics, and then try to attain your dream."

Next Williams determines the floor plan. She knows where the furniture is going to go and what is upholstered and what isn't. A good sofa is a necessity;

she advises clients to buy the best they can afford so they can keep it all their lives and just recover it when they want to. Then the ultimate shopper goes shopping, not sure what she's going to find. "I want my rooms to look as if my clients have been out every weekend having the best time collecting things they love," she remarks.

The usual result is a controlled riot of periods, colors, and patterns. A house looks as if it has evolved with a family over time, with plenty of places for needlepoint pillows and majolica. She likes a room with wonderful pictures, good furniture, and pretty rugs. But no one element should overpower the others. It's the complete picture that counts. "Great design is about all the elements coming together in harmony."

Williams is always exploring new color combinations, like pumpkin and saffron, or cinnamon and teal. "Color

Bunny Williams decorated this Federal-style house in Connecticut for a young family who wanted a livable elegance. ■ The ottoman and stool next to the Art Deco-style easy chairs maximize seating in the living room (opposite). ■ Rather than expensively framing the set of garden prints in the entrance hall (above), she cleverly mounted them on marbleized paper and glued them directly onto the striped wallpaper. ■ Another seating area in the living room (overleaf) focuses on a gilded wood coffee table. The shirred curtains are simple yet distinctive, designed with apronlike layers that are less fancy than a valance.

makes me happy," she says. "I don't do rooms where every last thing is white."

As with furniture, it's that blend of elements Williams is after. If a room is too studied, she thinks it gets boring. Taking one chintz and splashing it everywhere would be too predictable for this designer, who hoards vintage fabrics to toss into the mix, and doesn't think twice about upholstering Louis XVI chairs with faded toile bedspreads. In one dining room, she pasted eighty original paintings for plate designs on the walls, then topped off the composition with even more trompe l'oeil plates, urns, and brackets. "I love decoration," she declares, "and I'm not afraid of it."

Williams thinks her work is getting stronger and simpler. She was part of the New York firm of Parish-Hadley for more than twenty years before going off on her own, and it was an excellent education. What distinguishes her rooms is real-life common sense. There is always a table just where one would want to set a drink, and a good lamp by the perfect chaise. She tries to understand what will please her clients, as opposed to merely pleasing herself.

Williams hails from Virginia and has her share of southern charm. "I love furniture, I love houses, and I love entertaining, which is why it's easy for me to set it up for others," she says. "I know how people function in a house and what makes things work." She provides every accoutrement, down to the napkins — linen, not paper — for people who want to live well.

Three dining areas suit different moods. ■ Williams painted trompe l'oeil columns and balustrades instead of the typical lattice in the sunny garden room (above left) and put sisal matting on the floor. ■ The breakfast room (above right) off the kitchen is furnished with a country French table, swiveling steel chairs from the 1950s, and a handwoven cotton rug. A nineteenth-century Directoire needlepoint carpet sets the tone in the gracious dining room (opposite), where comfortable French chairs of the same period surround a mahogany Deco table.

Williams loves painted furniture, like the nineteenth-century Italian screen and the charming round table, an Italian Directoire design, in the apricot-tinted sitting room (opposite) off the master bedroom. ■ She enlarged the connecting door and constructed closets on either side (above) to make the division between the two rooms more attractive. The table next to the black lacquered bed is a copy of her own bedside table, which conveniently offers a shelf and a drawer.

VICENTE Wolf

MOST PEOPLE THINK VICENTE WOLF'S INTERIORS are all white. "They're not," says Wolf, with a mischievous grin. "But all my rooms have the freshness of white." He does take advantage of color, but it's color that's barely there, like shadows on snow. One has to look closely to see that the white is tinged with violet or blue gray or pink.

Wolf was only 16 years old when he arrived in America, a Cuban immigrant who had not even finished high school. He eventually found himself sweeping the floors in a fabric showroom. Three years later his first project was published in *House Beautiful.* "I knew exactly where I wanted to go," says the designer.

His distilled version of modern is sophisticated and spare without being cold. He looks to Japanese gardens, which find a Zen balance in imbalance, for inspiration. "I like to say what I want to say with the least amount of words," he explains.

By neutralizing the perimeter and keeping everything off the walls, Wolf expands a space so it appears to go on forever. This creates a feeling of emptiness and calm even in rooms with a full quota of furniture. Each piece has a strong presence because such bareness demands it. Grouped into families, the deliberately overscaled furniture anchors a room and manages to combine both comfort and elegance. Against Wolf's muted backgrounds, shape definitely matters. He embraces

The young couple who own this classic Manhattan apartment with high ceilings and fine moldings hired Vicente Wolf to update it. "It was a beautiful, traditional space, which I cleaned up and brought up to today without removing references to the past." ■ In the softly tinted living room, Wolf likes the graphic punch of a black-and-white photograph, blown up and hung off-center (opposite). ■ The barley-twist legs of an antique table are deliberately profiled against a pale couch (above). ■ A leaning mirror, Wolf's trademark, echoes the scale of the mantel (overleaf) while the ottoman below repeats the square proportions on a horizontal level. He irreverently slipcovered the eighteenth-century French chair and chose a simple sisal rug, believing the oriental carpet his clients initially preferred would have tipped the space too far back into formality.

opposites: classic Edwardian-style curves and crisp modern profiles; straight arms and rounded backs; tight upholstery and loose cushions. Mixing periods is part of the process. "As time goes by, certain points of view come into focus and others recede," says Wolf. "If five or ten years from now we're thinking traditional, then the more traditional pieces will draw attention." If he chooses antiques, he deploys them in a very modern way, silhouetting them against a bare wall like sculptures. "After all," says Wolf, "antiques were all modern at one time."

Color to this subtle alchemist is a blue so evanescent it almost evaporates: Vivid hues would be jarring. He returns again and again to taupe, caramel, beige, and creamy white. Touches of gold glinting off frames and dashes of black run through his rooms, linking everything together. With such a limited palette, surfaces take on an immense importance and the shift from smooth to rough, sheen to matte is carefully calibrated.

Wolf specializes in variations on a theme, intensified and refined through repetition. When he redecorated Richland, an 1848 Greek Revival plantation house in Natchez, Missisippi, he daringly chose a single fabric, carpet, and window treatment to connect the rooms and bring out the strong architecture. There was ambiguity to those spaces. They were both traditional and modern: much, perhaps, like the designer himself.

In the master bath, an almost invisible door opens in an ethereal frosted glass wall (above) to reveal a shower stall and makeup table. ■ Wolf will repeat certain materials — polished wool, textured linen, lustrous silk, sisal, slate — throughout a house like a reverberating chord. The library chairs (opposite), for example, pick up the darker leather that upholsters the living room ottoman. The black granite-topped table rises from cocktail level to dining height at the push of a button.

JOSEF SUDEK Zdeněk Kirschner TAKARAJIMA BOOKS

JACQUES
grange

JACQUES GRANGE CANNOT FOR THE LIFE OF HIM think of a single rule by which he mixes his audacious bouquets of antiques, fabrics, and paint. The only maxim that can possibly matter, he finally decides, is to combine many different things so that in their differences, they pulse. "The idea," he reflects, "is to generate life, poetry, humor, and gaiety."

Paris runs in the veins of this cultured and widely traveled citizen of the world. A son of the chic 16th arrondissement, Grange studied across town at the hands-on École Boulle among craftsmen, apprenticed with the great arbiter of taste, Henri Samuel, and became a close friend of the eccentric grande dame of Paris decorating,

Madeleine Castaing. From the late but revered Modernist master Jean-Michel Frank, he learned lessons of rigor and comfort, and from Castaing, the imperative of poetry in a room. Samuel taught him the basics. "He influenced me by his demand for quality and his classicism, which makes things timeless," recalls Grange.

Can two or more of these influences coexist in the same room? "Absolutely," maintains the designer. Indeed, *Le style Grange* results from the spontaneous combustion of disparate elements. He interprets tradition, culture, and classicism to adapt them to today's ideas, making rooms that are "comfortable, elegant, and rational."

Grange approaches a design by giving a room what he calls backbone. " I study

French designer Jacques Grange decorated his country retreat in Provence in a loose and comfortable artist's studio style inspired by the houses once maintained by Miró and Picasso in the same area. ▪ "I'm much more influenced by my travels than by the work of my colleagues," says the designer, who collected the ceramics in the kitchen (above) and the dining room (opposite) in the French Midi. A local craftsman fabricated the star-shaped metal light fixture, punctured with hundreds of pinholes. ▪ The living room (overleaf) exemplifies the Grange penchant for grand and fearless mixes. In front of the stone fireplace, a Louis XIII *fauteuil* made in the seventeenth century faces a pair of 1950s iron-and-rattan chairs by the French furniture maker Jean Royère. The rug is Berber, and the bull is a folkloric sculpture used in local festivals.

the porportions of a door and the molding to give points of architecture to the volume," he explains. If the light in a space is good, he enhances it. If the room is dark, he accentuates its somber character. "Never work against the nature of a room," Grange says. Avoiding conspicuous harmonies, he modulates each element for contrast. He opposes matte and polished surfaces, puts large objects in small rooms, creates intimate arrangements in large spaces. He believes in his objects and listens to the conversations they have together.

Although Grange's interiors do not resemble each other, each is swayed by the circumstances of the commission: the owner, the site, the country, the light. He listens to his clients' problems out of professionalism, and because their character adds another impulse to the mix. He is decorating's tightrope walker whose cultivated tastes are the only safety net for his daring.

Grange has furnished his low-ceilinged living room (above) — once a shed for sheep — with long, low pieces conceived by architects and designers during the first half of the century. ■ The Craftsman-style armchairs made of wood are by Jean Royère. ■ Tropical palm hangings by Boisseau that date from the 1930s and mosquito netting set an insouciant tone in the master bedroom (opposite top). ■ Provençal quilts in bold colors cover twin beds in a guest bedroom (opposite bottom). The armoire is an English Arts and Crafts piece, while the American flag is of World War I vintage. "I need to surprise myself with the unexpected," says the designer. "Creating, finally, means taking risks."

MARIETTE
himes gomez

IN ONE OF HER FIRST COURSES AT THE RHODE ISLAND School of Design, Mariette Himes Gomez was asked to draw something without lifting her pencil from the paper. "It was a good reminder that things should be continuous," she recalls. "A room is a volume. Your eye starts at one place and finishes at another. There should be a rhythm and a clarity of line. I think that's why I like circles," she adds. "The line is never broken and completes itself."

Gomez's rooms are as gracefully balanced as an equation. Furniture pieces have not forgotten their geometry lessons. One of her own chair designs features a wooden back incorporating a circle within a square. Square, flat ottomans that function as coffee tables are tightly upholstered in raffia cloth,

rather than tufted: The rectilinearity connotes a certain propriety. There is an impression of order, a disciplined hierarchy, and a no-nonsense attitude about objects in these rooms. "I'm in the school of those that take away," Gomez says. Yet her restraint never becomes rigid. "I can't seem to finish a room without overstuffing a sofa, or else it doesn't feel like home," she explains.

Her modernism has soft edges. Fundamentally, she believes in comfort and simplicity. The down-filled sofa, for example, is usually covered in vanilla chenille. Linen is another perennial favorite. "It's the most neutral of neutrals — the Zen of fabric," says Gomez, who also loves the pure lines of small, medium, or large stripes. "No matter how refined a room, I still want it to feel friendly and inviting," she says. Easy, yet elegant.

The layout of this long Manhattan drawing room is a lesson in design wisdom. Rather than using one central seating area that flows out into lesser eddies, Mariette Himes Gomez created two symmetrical groups in front of the twin fireplaces at either end. The mirror flanked by pictures over one mantel is reversed to become a picture flanked by mirrors over the other. Color is also part of the balancing act; in both groups, armchairs are unpholstered in green, sofas in cream. ■ A Georgian partner's desk bridges the gap, while Italian armchairs (opposite) float free to join any conversation. ■ Jewel-toned Steuben glass vases from the 1920s are silhouetted on a 1940s French table made of bronze (above).

A sofa and two upholstered chairs anchor the far end of the drawing room. The treatment of the two seating areas is similar, but the furniture styles are so different that the symmetry does not become boring. To suit the generous height of the ceiling and emphasize the pilasters, Gomez elongated the shafts of the French antique fireplace sconces and painted faux fluting behind them. With typical understatement, she left the mantel bare except for an amethyst silverina vase, placed off-center below a pen and ink drawing by Matisse. She was delighted to find one of her favorite talismans — the circle — carved in the center of the stone surround.

ALBERT
hadley

So imaginative, yet so simple. For more than forty years, Albert Hadley has created the kind of rooms that have defined the design field. His taut, svelte style provided the perfect counterpoint to the cachepots and voluptuous chintz so beloved by the late Sister Parish. When the two joined forces at Parish-Hadley in the early 1960s they set the gold standard of American decorating.

Hadley converses fluently in any idiom, from Park Avenue palatial to streamline moderne, but there are certain constants in his work. "I always try to respect and play up the architectural qualities of a space," he says. "Even empty rooms speak." Once he is pleased with the background, he can head in any direction. He will stop short, however, at turning an anonymous box into a Georgian fantasy. Appropriateness is his mantra.

Not above mixing the mundane with the grand, Hadley has been known to pick up furniture discarded on the street. The shape of a piece interests him more than its intrinsic value. He's drawn to objects with strong, sculptural lines that can hold their own and punctuate space. He considers the negative space around an object just as important as the object itself. "I'm interested in the skyline of a room — the ups and downs and the rhythm as you go around," says the designer.

Hadley is always trying something new. At one point he took all the furniture out of his living room except one round table and a few comfortable chairs — perfect for conversation, in his opinion. The plaster on the walls in his

Albert Hadley, head of one of the most prestigious decorating firms in the country, has lived in this modest Manhattan apartment for thirty years. He has revised and revamped the space over and over, while retaining the same basic palette: black and white with dashes of red. ■ Hadley, who loves sculptural shapes, set a red metal zigzag table next to his grandfather's tufted chaise in the living room (opposite). ■ The "sorcerer's apprentice" bookcase (above) was made of lacquered and decorated wood in Germany in the 1920s. ■ The designer built out the walls in the living room (overleaf) to eliminate ugly columns and provide secret storage space, then mirrored the recess at the ceiling line and baseboard so the walls would appear to float.

own apartment is flecked with mica dust, so it sparkles in the light. Designer Sybil Connolly once gave him a piece of carved and gilded wood molding set with big button rhinestones, salvaged from one of Ireland's great country houses. This find would inspire one of the most glamorous New York City dining rooms of the decade: Hadley upholstered the walls in damask and recreated this molding, running it under the cornice, along the baseboards, and all around the doors, as if the room were wearing a diamond necklace. Van Day Truex, the former head of Parsons School of Design in New York, where Hadley studied and still teaches, told him once that a room should *growl*. "I like a little bit of naughtiness in a room. Not every space has to be austere," says the designer.

The soft-spoken gentleman dean of American decorating used to design clothes for his sister's paper dolls back in Nashville. "I've always loved painting, drawing, costumes, feathers, tinsel, houses, cars, and furs," he recalls. "I was playing with materials then, and here I am, still doing it." The latest crop of decorators speaks of him with awe. How does he manage to keep his work eternally young, fresh, and exciting? "I'm constantly on the move, looking at everything, and I'm enormously inquisitive," is his answer.

"I am a very precise person," says Hadley, and it shows. ■ Straight from the catalogue, the L.L. Bean blanket on his bed (above) is as tightly tucked as a drill sergeant's. He removed the pillows because they would spoil the line of the flat plane. ■ This supremely sophisticated man chose primary colors — tomato red, sapphire blue, and taxicab yellow — to cover 1920s chairs in his dining room (opposite), which migrate to other rooms as needed. The celestial blue wall panel is actually a painted corkboard, where Hadley can change his art collection on a whim. Bored with plain ceilings, he painted this one dark, to unify the space.

NANCY
braithwaite

Atlanta decorator Nancy Braithwaite considers a job successful when a client walks into one of her rooms and sighs. With a few impeccably chosen American antiques she creates an interior world possessing that same limpid stillness, laden with meaning, found in a painting by Vermeer. Her plain-spoken designs have a Shakerlike simplicity and a sober power derived from the strength and integrity of the unadorned primitive furnishings she favors. This is country style without sentimentality.

Once she gets the architecture right, Braithwaite likes to build a room around a distinctive piece of furniture that provides a center of gravity: in her own living room it was a six-foot-long sawbuck table made in the 1700s.

Next, the designer works out her palette. "Color tells you how to feel in a room," she says. "I really like dusty, muted shades; I can't live with bright yellow." Her hand-mixed hues — cinnamon, pale bird's-egg blue, buttermilk, smoky charcoal, oatmeal, muddy green, and tobacco brown — seem to sponge up the sunlight. Along with the antiques, these murky, ambiguous colors are what actually give her rooms their feeling of age, creating dark corners and mysterious shadows. She never lets the blazing sun violate the illusion: Light is filtered and controlled.

Entering one of Nancy Braithwaite's rooms sometimes feels like stepping into a primitive painting. ■ The muddy green-blue eighteenth-century wainscot she added in the dining room of this house in the North Carolina mountains typifies her dusky palette and sets the tone for the rest of the paint (opposite). She started with the red chairs and then chose the simplest "red-black-brown" table she could find. ■ The tall hunt board (above) is a form indigenous to the South. ■ Braithwaite wanted her clients to feel as if they were outside when sitting on the glass-enclosed porch (overleaf) so she purposely brought nature's colors indoors. The antique wicker lamps were so tall she commissioned linen undercloths for them so the light wouldn't shine in anyone's eyes. Bamboo matchstick blinds, dyed dark brown, filter the glare from the sun, while rough burlap covers the round table and plays off the textures of the wicker furniture.

If there is no architecture in a room and no budget to invent some, Braithwaite's strategy is to go straight to the draperies to create some structure. Sheer organdy curtains at the windows gently puddle on the floor. Fabric with a handwoven look appeals to her. Burlap has been a recent passion; she made hangings for her own bed from the coarse, raw material, then attached a fine starched white handkerchief linen lining detailed with tiny antique buttons. She loves texture and plays of texture. She uses cotton so soft and worn that it has the feel of old paper money, and lets silk velvet flirt with flannel.

"Color and texture are the great unifiers," says Braithwaite, and they bind her rooms into seamless compositions shaped by good lines and pure form. Accessories are left until last. "You shouldn't have to rely on them to make a room happen," she maintains. If a room doesn't look quite right, she will take all the accessories out, and then put them back one by one. After each addition she steps back, and stops when the room holds her eye. There is not one extraneous object. Her own sawbuck table is bare. She deals with the essentials. "I think I'm trying to get closer to the bone," she says.

Because her client had a large collection of objects and wanted them all around her, these rooms are less lean and spare than Braithwaite's usual interiors, but still reveal her characteristic sense of serenity. When the owner saw the finished design, she said she felt as if someone had just put their arms around her. ■ Prints, including Audubon turkeys, are gathered into a striking composition over a desk (above left). ■ Layering pattern on texture, a tapestry pattern borders tobacco-colored linen curtains (above right). ■ This relatively new house needed an injection of character, so Braithwaite, working with architect Norman Askins, brought in the antique beams and fireplace to anchor the living room (opposite top). ■ In the family room, Askins sheathed black-painted walls with 1-by-10 boards to add instant character (opposite bottom).

CHRISTIAN liaigre

FIRST, HE CREATES THE QUIET. "YOU MUST CLEAN AND purify a room, taking away the small and superficial to establish the void," says French designer Christian Liaigre. "Then bring in just a few objects made only from beautiful materials."

Liaigre — who loves the country-side and would have stayed there had he passed the tests to become a veterinarian — has practiced on his own in Paris for a decade, assembling resonant, refined interiors that disci-pline the Gallic predilection for *luxe, calme,* and *volupté.* His work evolves from the spare and elegant, yet still relaxed, tradition of French Modernism set out by Jean-Michel Frank in the 1920s, and he acknowledges a deep respect for the designer and architect Pierre Chareau, the Giacometti broth-ers, and his great inspiration, sculptor Constantin Brancusi. Their combined influences impart a certain serenity to his rooms. "We need calm to make homes into harbors from the chaos of our offices and streets," says Liaigre. "Some people do it with a baroque decor, and others with a decor much more strict than mine. My handwriting is peaceful, not tortured."

In France, with its long tradition of interior design, decorators are awash in precedent, and Liaigre, trained at the École Nationale Supérieure des Arts Décoratifs, walks a fine line between a shared design past and individual free-dom. He believes that all these influ-ences register, as in a computer, and then there's the moment

Christian Liaigre walks through a conventional Paris courtyard to get to his late-nineteenth-century house, but beyond the front door all conformity stops. ■ The French designer invited artist Pierre Bonnefille to make a painting directly on the dining room wall (opposite); the luminous result has the improvisatory impact of jazz. Liaigre designed almost all the furniture in the house himself, including the slatted console and a dining table of African wenge wood. ■ The chair (above), carved in sycamore, is a prototype designed for a Parisian hotel by Liaigre, who recast the traditional proportions of a Louis XVI *fauteuil* to emphasize the sinuous limbs. ■ The tongue-in-cheek painting above the leather couch in the living room (overleaf) is made with the gold leaf normally used on frames; here it is applied to the canvas itself. Other artwork includes a fourth-century Asian head and photographs by Nadar Fils of African ruins. The metal side chair is by Eric Schmitt.

for scanning all the memories and precedents, along with all the other considerations, like place, clients, and the light. "But I can never predict the moment," says Liaigre. "I strongly believe in the power of intuition."

Liaigre follows no recipes. He builds an atmosphere out of the emptiness and uses very little color, very little fabric, and never any printed materials. His palette is monochromatic and comes out of natural materials, such as leathers and woods. He designs furniture tailored to each commission, crafted to reveal the inherent beauty of sycamore, white oak, ebony, or African wenge. Clean and decisive lines set an influential precedent for simplicity, elegance, and strength.

The exceptional object — an African statue, a Thai buddha — reflects the influence of Liaigre's frequent travels in Africa and Asia. He believes that the architectural solidity and scale defining his interiors (sofas look like built-in banquettes and closets form entire walls) reveal lingering rustic tastes. "I was raised in the country, so I like things that are rooted," he says.

Although he occasionally uses a shock of color like lipstick red or royal blue for accent, he minimizes contrasts so that all parts defer to the whole. Nuanced lighting also plays a supporting role. He never uses harsh lights like halogen, which would break the spell, and filters artificial light with paper to preserve what he calls "atmospheric unity" and sustain the mood.

"In a monk's cell, there is a table, a bed and then the cross, that's all," he says. "It's the same for a house — find what is essential and refine it."

Liaigre travels widely, collecting objects as he goes; over the desk (above) he has hung a long, pencil-thin lake canoe used by the people of Karala, India. Artist Pierre Bonnefille painted a stripe with chevron ends directly on the study wall. With the boat, it ties the room together and conveys the calm associated with the horizontal line. ■ Venetian blinds (opposite) filter the light and give the room scale, a sense of horizontality, and a 1940s cast. A one-armed *méridienne* for napping waits beside Liaigre's desk; solid oak legs support an ebony top.

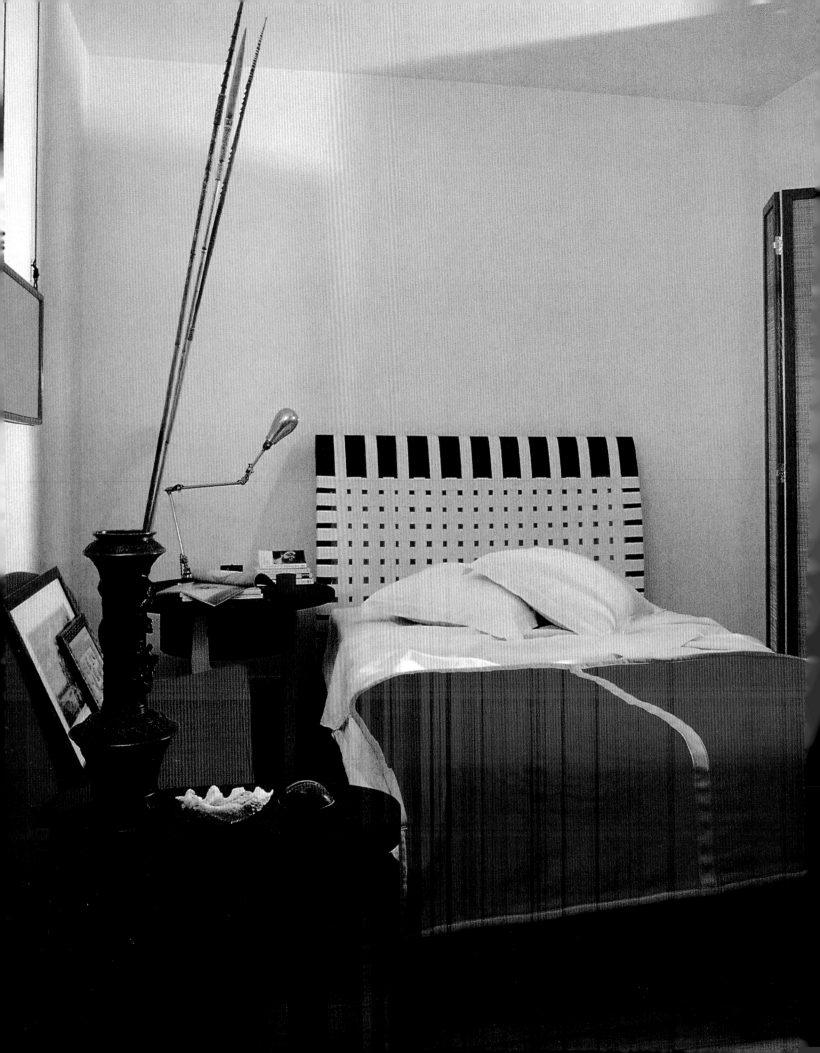

Liaigre created a serene environment with floor-to-ceiling, wall-to-wall oak closets in the skylit dressing room of his master suite (left). ■ Sea grass matting covering the floor extends into the master bedroom (below). The iroko-and-chestnut chair is a prototype for a design commissioned by the Club Med in Bora Bora. Irish linen curtains on a wrought-iron rail provide a backdrop for a Noguchi lamp with a rice paper shade.

The centerpiece of the guest bedroom is the oak bed, painted with india ink and finished with a headboard woven of cotton webbing (opposite). The crimson horse blanket used as a coverlet picks up the reds from the camelback sofa and the Vietnamese mirror frame.

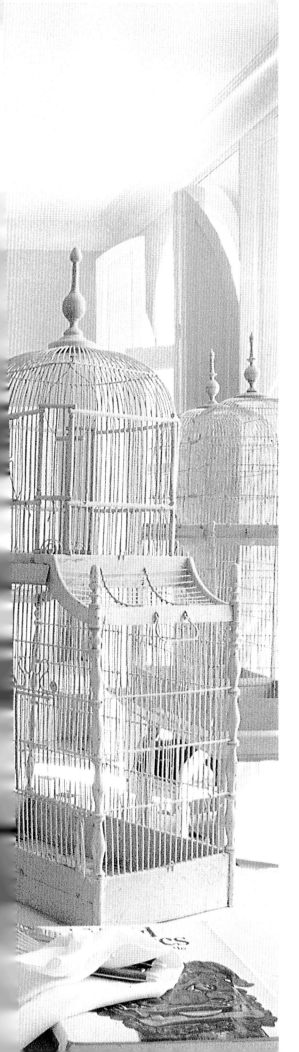

A ● SENSE OF
design

WHETHER THE IDEA OR THE FURNITURE COMES FIRST, HAVING something to say and the skills to express it are prerequisites for successful interiors. A good design is usually the fusion of a thousand and one impulses. To achieve cohesion when so many elements are involved in putting a room together, there must be a specific point of view.

SIMPLICITY IS ONE APPROACH TO ELOQUENCE. MORE PEOPLE are paring down to essentials so the individuality of each object in a room has a strong presence within the whole. Balance is another basic principle of any composition. In his Newport gallery, for example, designer Robert Hill exploited classical symmetry to create an atmosphere of elegance and repose. That sort of balance is crucial to a well-tempered interior. Forget it and the fabled mix becomes a mess.

OR DOES IT? FOR EVERY DESIGN MAXIM, THERE IS SOMEONE to break it. Those brave enough to defy convention often produce the most delightful rooms. Many professionals recommend taking chances. "Decorating is not some mystery," says seasoned designer Albert Hadley. "It's the expression of personality. Don't be afraid of making a mistake. You can always change it."

STRIKING A
balance

ROOMS, LIKE THE GALAXY, ARE SUBJECT TO NEWTONIAN law: For every design action, there is an equal and opposite reaction. Ideally, their sum total balances in the end. The cohesiveness of a composition depends on the relationships of the various elements in a room.

Contrast and harmony are both valid approaches. A severe, straight-laced chair, for example, might want something relaxed and cozy, like an overstuffed sofa, nearby. Coordinated colors, patterns, and textures, in turn, create a soothing synthesis of design.

But balance is not merely a question of matching fabrics. A good decorator also looks for spatial equilibrium. Symmetry is a tried-and-true solution: two chairs opposite a sofa; candlesticks on either side of the dining table with a bowl of flowers in between. But sometimes asymmetry is more interesting. A single vase instead of the conventional pair might be set on a mantel. Three seashells, several family photographs, or nothing at all might hold down the other side. It's all a matter of instinct, and knowing just when to move that vase on the mantel two inches over.

Four square pavilions — one just a sheltered terrace — balance open and enclosed spaces in a seaside retreat on the French Riviera. ■ In the entry between the living and dining pavilions (opposite), Italian architect Gae Aulenti used buff-colored walls, sandstone floors, and wood painted the azure blue of the sea to blur the boundaries between indoors and out. Opposing twin staircases punctuate the strong vertical symmetry of French doors, which turn the spare interior into a vessel of light, open to every breeze. ■ Instead of typical French country furniture, quixotic antique chairs in a Renaissance design float within the space, hot flashes of scarlet that offset the cool scheme. Dispersed around an Eero Saarinen dining table designed in the 1950s (above), they look like figures in a modern minuet.

The couple who share this eighteenth-century stone manor house in rural France fell in love with it because it feels like a small château. But formality was not part of the picture when they decorated the high-ceilinged salon with a blithe mix of furniture and objets d'art, some serious and some serendipitous. The balance comes from a deliberate contrast of style and century. ■ In front of a regal Empire settee (opposite top) the coffee table is a common slab of stone, set on hollow flue tiles. ■ In a similar gesture of confident nonchalance, cotton bed-sheets are thrown over the sofas next to the elegant Louis XV fireplace (opposite bottom). ■ The whimsical 1950s coat rack (above left) becomes a sculpture in its own right, given just as much prominence as the polished black marble bust (above right) that echoes the voluptuous curves of an Art Deco easy chair.

With art as vigorous as this, one choice is to neutralize the setting and let the pieces be the focus of the room. In a Florida house, interiors designed by Hal Martin Jacobs defer to the client's rollicking contemporary collection and establish a bold architectural scale that allows the art to breathe. ■ Blond wood in the master bedroom (opposite) is a quiet foil to Ray Brandt's boisterous *Homage to Matisse* screen. ■ The breakfast area (above) is cool white, except for Mies van der Rohe's modern classic, the Barcelona chair, which looks like a slash of black straight out of one of the multicolored Keith Haring prints. Stacked in a grid that mimics the window pattern, the prints attain a scale suitable to the double-height space. The white Eero Saarinen table and Arne Jacobsen chairs are design classics from the 1950s, still in production today.

This profusion of pattern is not for the faint-hearted. Once designer Michael Stanley committed himself to 100 yards of cabbage rose printed cotton, which pull together the wall planes of his meandering living room, four small rooms now merged into one, he had to equilibrate the rest of the space. ■ To do so, he waged war with even more pattern. Graphic gingham upholstery and a checkerboard floor (above left) stand up well to the floral bouquets. ■ Stanley upped the ante with a nineteenth-century ratchet sofa covered in a quivering vine pattern (above right). ■ Occasional swathes of solid color do relieve the eye, however: A green linen-velvet sofa is entrenched in one of the three different seating areas (opposite top). ■ An upholstered three-seater in red — the complement of green — helps balance the scheme (opposite bottom).

paring
DOWN

heightens the melody, empty space, neutral walls, or bare floors allow a room and the furniture in it to breathe. Design today is more often a matter of subtraction rather than addition as rooms are reduced to a few good pieces that are all the more striking surrounded by space. In the feverish 1980s, more was better and plethora best, but now people feel sated. Even in rooms that thrive on abundance, the idea is to discipline and distill the parts to achieve an ensemble that reads as a whole.

Paring down often means that the best features of a room become more prominent: the moldings, the mantel, the honey-colored parquet. Good editing, however, does not mean that the furnishings should be stripped down to a futon and a single tulip in an ovoid vase. It can be as simple as keeping the horizon line of the furniture low to let the architectural elements of the room emerge. Clarity is the first commandment. Jettison anything that breaks a mood or contradicts an idea. What is left out may be just as important as what is left in.

There are only a few pieces of furniture in this serene living room, and no strident colors, simply the gleam of burnished wood against white. ■ The mix of cultures is intriguing, with a Louis Philippe chair drawn up to an Early American table (opposite). When the owner of this 1916 Connecticut house arrived in New York as a young man, he met an antiques dealer who advised him to buy only the best, a philosophy he has followed ever since. Whenever this discriminating collector — who dips into a span of periods — gathers a multitude of objects, they are a variation on a single theme, like the array of tenth-century Sung dynasty tea bowls. ■ The curvaceous French sofa offers a nice contrast to the stripped-down, straight-edged, decidedly Calvinist mantel (above).

In this elegantly edited Parisian dining room, a table shaped to echo a wine keg and a quartet of distinctively flared chairs manage to look archaic and modern at the same time (above). ■ Four oversize photographs are clustered for impact rather than dispersed across the walls. In the same house, the graphic pattern of the wrought-iron spiral staircase against white walls (opposite) turns it into a sculptural element, the industrial equivalent of the art objects displayed on the mantel. Refined choices are a hallmark of the room's designer, Christian Liaigre, whose genius lies in the way he arranges a few elemental objects in chaste rooms to striking effect. Like a work of primitive art that simply concentrates on the bare basics of a figure, his ensembles are pared down to the bone. That spareness helps show off the exotic grain of a wood or the hand-carved curve of a table.

Nancy Braithwaite took the cute out of country with her finely honed version of America's homegrown style. A few fine primitive pieces anchor her own Atlanta living room, including the tall Georgia hunt board at the window and the sawbuck table between the down-filled sofas upholstered in creamy matelassé. Instead of compromising the table by cutting it down to coffee-table height, she built the custom-made couches up. "It gives the room even more power when you scale things up," she says. By keeping the walls and upholstery the same shade of buttermilk, Braithwaite quieted the room and let the strong lines stand out.

John Saladino understood the soul of the prim, patrician clapboard Colonial house, built in 1762. Instead of gussying it up, he scraped it down to its good, graceful New England bones. Bare walls, bare floors, and bare windows conjure the innocent austerity of an earlier era. ■ In the front sitting room (opposite) he stripped away centuries of paint and paper to reveal the old mottled plaster, nacreous as the inside of an oyster shell. The eye focuses on a few intriguing pieces — a nineteenth-century black tole tray table, Italian leather chairs made in the 1700s — and pristine slipcovers in white linen neutralize the rest of the furniture. ■ A quilt draped over a table provides the backdrop for an evocative still life (above), combining the humble and the rare.

DEFYING
convention

BLESSED ARE THE CHEFS WHO CAN COOK EXTRAORDINARY meals without recipes. Many designers also create never-before, never-again rooms instinctively, ignoring convention and even flouting it. For these great souls of the interior there are no rules, only freedom: They glide past decorating disasters on the strength of the eye. Utterly imperturbable, they might leave peeling plaster on the walls, or declare their independence with jarring juxtapositions of pattern, startling shifts of scale, and marginal colors. This is take-no-prisoners decorating. These rooms have attitude.

For those who have the nerve to scrawl polka dots on a tangerine wall, there is no going back to building a room around paint chips and fabric swatches painstakingly chosen to match the carpet. Creating the unexpected, however, requires knowing what is expected. Picasso had to learn to draw like an Old Master before he could leave all that behind. Invention is far riskier than convention, and at its best reveals the individual behind the interior. That's double exposure, but do anything less and the thrill is gone.

No one standing outside this 1840 Pennsylvania German farmhouse in Bucks County would ever suspect what lurks within. ▪ Next to the living room fireplace there is a purple velvet chair (opposite) with a tail dragging on the plank floor like some lumbering sea creature. The owners, furniture designers Sergio and Monique Savarese, concocted this chair and the rest of the menagerie. To show them off, they whited out walls and ceiling to create a crisp, gallerylike atmosphere for pieces that seem to have dropped in from another planet. ▪ In the study (above) the original horsehair-stiffened plaster, raw and cracked, is the perfect backdrop for their neo-primitive Dream Screen made of rush and carved maple wood.

The seriousness of fine antiques in this prestigious setting created by Barbara Wirth and her cousin and partner, decorator Christian Badin, is constantly subverted by insouciance. In the most classic of Parisian apartments, with double-height ceilings, an enfilade of doors, and moldings galore, the designers decided to break with convention and take decorating lightly. ■ Painted wood cypress trees surrounded by a herd of watering cans strike the first note of wit in the entrance hall (opposite), paved with stone and black marble cabochon insets. Instead of setting one blue glass vase on the dining room mantel (above right), Wirth gathered dozens; the more stems, the merrier. ■ In summer, the scheme changes and clear glass populates the same mantel (right).

The designers of these dining rooms put a twist on the expected by pulling up sofas to the tables rather than conventional chairs. ▪ Sandra Nunnerley chose a sky blue banquette big enough to stretch out on over coffee and the morning newspaper for an apartment in the Bahamas (above). ▪ The shock of dandelion yellow pillows against the Yves Klein-blue settee in a Savannah dining room designed by Vicente Wolf (opposite) should start a lively conversation. By inviting Queen Anne–style armchairs and bow-tied slipper chairs to join the double pedestal table, he made the seating arrangement as idiosyncratic as the guests.

Banana branches may not hang in most Manhattan dining rooms, but in this one a single saturated paint color — pistachio — wafts the space straight to the tropics. New York designers Laura Bohn and Joseph Lembo saw no reason why reproductions of traditional English mahogany furniture should always look sedate, so they livened things up with citric color to create rooms that might have been owned by an English planter in the Caribbean. ■ Rather than mounted on the wall in the usual manner, a framed "ancestor" rests on the floor behind a shield-back chair with studded upholstery (opposite). ■ The sweep of the curtain — very architectural, with bold horizontal stripes — becomes even more dramatic when tied with rope (above right). ■ Chippendale-style side chairs surround the dining table, while a comfortable wing chair commands the head (right).

Instead of trying to "fix up" and modernize this 1890 stone house built by an Italian grape farmer in Connecticut, the designer took the structure down to its primitive bones. ■ In the living room (left), Charles Spada peeled off eight layers of linoleum and newspaper to reveal wide pine floorboards, then furnished the space with a mix of traditional antiques that were undoubtedly startled when the 1950s tiger-striped chairs arrived. ■ Most of the plaster was scraped from the walls in the dining room (above), where sturdy English oak chairs surround a painted Swedish table.

Even in Charleston, South Carolina, where they appreciate a crumbling ruin, some think architect Randolph Martz has gone too far. Never mind the peeling paint in his 1851 house; there are gaping holes in the ceiling, unfinished floors, and raw swathes of plaster where he tore down a dividing wall. Martz dislikes the sort of restorations that wipe out a house's history; instead he layered the rooms with more vestiges of time. ■ Not all relate specifically to their new location. The originals of the plaster casts (above) reside in the Louvre. ■ Cast-iron brackets and balusters are clustered near the stairs (opposite, top left). ■ More collections of oddities, like fragments of Roman amphorae (opposite, top right) and old fireplace tongs (opposite, bottom left), also populate the rooms. ■ Models of unbuilt houses in Martz's office (opposite, bottom right) reveal a classical bent.

A SENSE OF
craft

WHETHER THE SETTING IS SWEDISH COUNTRY OR STILETTO-
sharp Streamline Moderne, what inevitably draws the eye is
the touch of the hand. Furnishings and architectural elements
that carry the mark of their maker — as in the graceful arc of a
fine-boned Windsor chair — bring personality into the house .

NO PURCHASE IS REQUIRED, UNLESS A BRUSH AND A FEW CANS
of paint count. That's all Vincent Dané needed to transform
his rustic French farmhouse into a not-to-be-forgotten retreat.
One day, inspired by Matisse, he spontaneously brushed stylized
oak leaves across the plaster walls of the drawing room.

PAINT, HOWEVER, IS JUST ONE OF THE TANTALIZING CHOICES.
A good designer knows the possibilities inherent in fabric,
wood, stone, and metal, as well. Each has its own particular
character: Consider the voluptuous drape of silk taffeta, the
mellow luster of antique paneling, the majesty of marble,
the stark sheen of aluminum. Today's stylemakers may take
Fauvist colors or stainless steel to a new level, but their flights
of fantasy are usually grounded in meticulous craftsmanship.
Any of these alluring elements, applied with care and originality,
can become the focal point of a distinctive room.

fabric
TRANSFORMATIONS

As Scarlett O'Hara and every designer know, personal destiny and the fate of houses can hang on a curtain. Dressing an individual and dressing a room have much in common: Fabric can trans- form a wallflower, or a wall. When deftly crafted, fabric is an indispensable tool in the designer's hand, capable of manip- ulating light, striking a mood, evoking a sense of place and time, and providing detail and texture. Lemon-yellow voile draped at the windows will make a room seem suffused with sun even on a cloudy day. Lustrous taffeta, embossed damask, iridescent silk, and gossamer gauze all have tremendous powers of connotation, conjuring the rich and strange. Distinctive patterns instantly whisk a room to faraway places: An adventurous designer might juxtapose a kaleidoscopic African batik, a woven Berber wool, and a striped French silk, playing anthropologist among these overlapping cultures. Passementerie delights and holds the eye, while plush velour and luscious chenille demand to be touched.

Starting with Roman shades made of hand-tinted tropical mesh, which suffuse the sunlight with amber, every fabric in this living room casts the space in a warm glow. To enhance the effect, designer Paul Siskin kept each textile within the same tonal range of cinnamon, umber, burnt sienna, copper, clove, and coffee brown. ■ The tribal patterns of the African kuba cloth covering the pillows (opposite) — along with Japanese kimono fabric and a Guatemalan blanket — transport visitors to distant continents. The sofas are covered in a corduroy chenille, and even the rug has a pronounced and unusual texture, which plays off the graphic stitching on the drapery borders (above).

Slipcovers can leapfrog centuries, cam-
ouflage shortcomings, and alter style.
■ Victoria Hagan covered a white-painted
bergère (left) in natural linen, which
homogenizes the shape of the piece
and makes it look almost contemporary.
George Washington's initials appliquéd
on the pillow add a touch of wit.

In designer Eve Robinson's Manhattan
bedroom (right), the armchair is all
dressed up for staying at home. Crisply
detailed with matching piping, the two-
toned upholstery fits tightly; the solid
planes of the amply proportioned chair
show off the fabric pattern and the
pleasing lines of the piece itself.

In Salle Werner Vaughn's turn-of-the-century Houston cottage, ordinary bent-wood chairs are suddenly Cinderellas, dressed for the ball in inexpensive drapery-lining fabric. The craft is in the detail and application: Loose box pleats are folded into feminine skirts that transform the seats into pretty slipper chairs, while gold braid becomes as important as elegant dressmaking trim. Contrasting welting details the upholstered pieces to make a statement of tailored simplicity.

Textiles can also have a major environmental impact, softening hard surfaces and muffling sound. Even a small dose, such as harlequin-patterned seat cushions used around a dining table, will punctuate a decor. And it doesn't have to cost a fortune to create a fantastic look. Designer John Saladino, for example, favors unbleached muslin, which he gently drapes over a window to create a soft dip in the middle. Caught at the upper corners of the window frame with two nails the size of railroad spikes, the humble fabric gracefully tumbles to the floor, overlapping by an inch and a half. Economical elegance.

The only limit to the versatility of fabric is the imagination. Hanging a canopy frame with tea-dyed linen bestows instant pedigree on a bed. Handsomely trimmed, snug uphol-stery brings out the strong lines of a structured sofa, while slipcovers hide any number of flaws and can make over a pedestrian chair into a debu-tante dressed for the cotillion. There are as many ways to tailor a piece of furniture as there are to tailor a suit, and a good deco-rator knows the kindest cuts of all.

With a length of fabric and a few tacks, Frédéric Méchiche performs feats of fancy in his seventeeth-century cottage in Provence. ■ Here's a lesson in the life of sev-eral blue stripes (above): strict and rectilinear at the service of a high-back chair, jaunty on down pillows, and elegant as a swag caught with three well-placed tacks. ■ Fabric is also having a fling in the main bedroom (opposite), seductively draped and fluid, reveling in its own fall, conforming to no rule. Méchiche noticed this particular drapery design on an eighteenth-century ex-voto in a local church and mimicked it with garnet-red Louis XV toile, which reappears on the side chair.

Superb detailing, evident in the fluted pleats and rolled piping, underscores the sense of luxury in this Parisian bedroom. The effect is enhanced by the glorious collage of pattern: a stripe, a solid, a floral, and even an exuberant pinwheeling quilt motif. The gorgeous array of fabric works because each is vibrant enough to hold its own — not surprising, since all are by Manuel Canovas, known for the sumptuous, unusual fabrics he designs.
■ One of his distinctive overscale prints — Pali, a botanical inspired by a visit to California — covers the walls and is draped at the window (opposite).
■ Canovas also designed the sheets, in a pattern called Ruban Rose (above).

FINE
woodworking

of building materials, wood is many things to many houses: structure, surface, and trim; texture, color, and grain; line, edge, and finish. Few building materials confer as much character on a house or a piece of furniture so dependably, and express so directly the imprint of the hand.

Craftsmen have spent centuries mastering wood's mysterious nature, and they can coax the most sinuous curves from its malleable limbs. Some artisans, especially the Japanese, simply let wood be, unobtrusively revealing the inherent beauty of the grain as decoration enough. Lately, more restless imaginations are challenging traditional treatments, bending and cutting wood into surreal fantasies. Designers on the edge are updating the stalwart traditions of stenciled floors and painted furniture. Tantalizing in its variety, wood can be stained and colored with myriad finishes — up to and including the provocative alkaline

The warmth of wood infuses the dining room of a circa 1840 Pennsylvania German farmhouse (opposite), a study of strong, durable craftsmanship, old and new. The plank floors and hand-carved raised paneling provide the old; Monique and Sergio Savarese, the furniture designers who own the house, provide the new. Their Malindi table is made of African anigré wood, with legs hand-turned to a contemporary shape. Conceived on a trip to Bali, the solid-back chair features a swirling "grain" pattern, printed on a wet finish with sliced coconut shells. ■ One fine detail — the jigsawn stringer pattern on the stairs — expresses all the care that went into this 1789 Federal house built in Fall River, Massachusetts (above).

dyes that transform the obviously natural into the conspicuously artificial: Lipstick-red floors anyone?

When people speak of a room's features, it is usually such elements as wood moldings, mantels, and balustrades that have caught their eye. These are the details that make the difference between a flat, uninteresting interior and one with physiognomy. Since wood is often used at points of transition — where a wall meets a ceiling or a window or a door — it accentuates the architecture with a flourish. The high priest of the profession, Frank Lloyd Wright, blurred the distinction between house and furniture with built-in banquettes, window seats, and cupboards that carried the line of the structure to places where skin touched the building. As he discerned, wood is not only visually rich, it is tactile. No other material offers quite the same sense of shaking hands with a house.

In Frank Lloyd Wright's hands, wood was like butter. He could make it do anything. Cypress serves as structure, shelter, and decoration in the 1940 Pope-Leighey house in Falls Church, Virginia, designed as part of Wright's effort to provide low-cost, intelligent housing for the middle class. Rooted in the earth, his concept of organic architecture was influenced by the Arts and Crafts movement and Japanese design, celebrating indigenous craftsmanship and materials. The virtue of cypress was that the house required so little maintenance on the interior — no paint, no plaster; just a bit of wax. On the outside, Wright let it weather. ■ The strong horizontal planes of the flat, cantilevered roof (above) extend the house into the landscape. ■ Cut-out windows (opposite) suggest sun-dappled shadows and the leafy tracery of the forest floor.

The graphic grid of door frames, window frames, shutters, shelves, trellises, and *brises-soleil* — all handcrafted of Douglas fir — provides a weightless counterpoint to the thick white masonry walls of this summer retreat on Sardinia. ■ In the simple 1,000-square-foot house, designed by architects Kathryn Ogawa and Gilles Depardon, screens and sliding doors differentiate one large space into parts, including the kitchen (opposite top), where Japanese pottery looks right at home in the Japanese-influenced aesthetic. ■ In the living area (opposite bottom), wood serves as both ornament and structure. ■ Pocket doors can shut off the bedroom from the living/dining/kitchen area (above left). ■ Interior and exterior spaces flow together since all rooms, including the bedroom (top right) open to terraces and views.

THE LOOK OF
stone

STONE, THE OLDEST OF DOMESTIC MATERIALS, HAS sheltered man since the cave, and from antiquity emerged as one of the most noble and venerable materials used in architecture. Available in elemental and highly refined forms, it spans the continents from cottage to castle. Small boulders gathered from fields or streams and nestled together in a chimneypiece declare the affinity of the house with nature. Marble, limestone, and sandstone have been lovingly carved for centuries into mantels with the grace of sculpture.

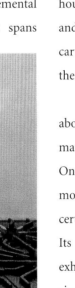

There is something satisfying about stone's sense of weight and permanence. It even improves with age. Once used structurally, today stone is more often applied as decoration, at certain special moments in a design. Its beauty is inherent. Marble often exhibits an aqueous quality, as though rivers ran through it before becoming petrified. Slate has a rippling texture. Limestone possesses the translucency of skin. When backlit, an onyx wall glows. Not merely pretty, stone also happens

Concrete may not be anyone's first thought for countertops, but California designer Fu-Tung Chen takes this inexpensive material and makes it look precious simply by design. ■ For his own kitchen counters (opposite) he built molds, lined them with plastic, then poured in his special formula of portland cement, gravel and sand, mixed with ultramarine and black pigments. Turquoise chips, fossils, and a bright green Gumby figure were embedded in the sludge just for fun. A custom-made chopping board slides along the built-in draining board from sink to sink and Douglas fir cabinets fit under the counter rather than above, where Cheng prefers windows. ■ Used as a counter surface, the poured concrete, smooth as velvet to the touch (above), conveys the same sense of immutability as stone.

to be practical. Bluestone wears well underfoot. Granite, durable and heat resistant, is preferred for kitchen countertops; pastry chefs favor cool, sleek marble slabs for rolling out dough. In recent years, improved stone-cutting techniques have made thin veneers and tiles possible, reducing the price of stone and and making it more accessible. Common concrete, an aggregate of stone, is another possibility; colored, poured, and polished, it looks sensational.

Once a bland, boxy apartment desperately seeking character, this Manhattan apartment (above) was rescued by designers Tom Fox and Joe Nahem. They covered the floors with bluestone tiles — instant texture — and mixed ocher, pewter, and white pigments into wet plaster for a marbleized effect — instant antiquity — on the walls. The gray wall behind the urn-shaped finial screens the front door. ▪ In a Connecticut guesthouse (opposite), John Saladino chose bluestone for the floors to give a new building an aura of age. Scratch-coat plaster walls mimicking the texture of stone convey a patina of time that comes naturally to the corroded cast-iron seashell tray embedded above the mantel.

Nothing is more elemental than stone, and a stone fireplace instantly anchors a room and provides a natural focal point. ■ In a Parisian apartment (opposite), Christian Liaigre let the stark black mantel speak for itself. The extra avoirdupois of the bowed console brackets only accentuates the attenuated lines of the Liaigre-designed lamps. ■ The Victorian mantel in a stately New Orleans home (above left) decorated by Ann Holden and Ann Dupuy exemplifies stone transformed, carved into a bounty of marble grape leaves as lush and inviting as the furnishings. ■ Sleek lines define an Art Deco mantel in a Manhattan penthouse living room (above right), revealing the marble in all its veined glory.

metal
WORKS

the unexpected edge. Designers are moving way beyond traditional touches of gold and silver: A sheet of steel makes an unforgettable fireplace or a commanding foyer wall.

There's a reason. Most people are attracted to something shiny, like birds snatching bits of stray tinsel to feather their nest. In a room softened with upholstery and carpets, the gleam of metal is enticing. Whether found in a traditional silver bowl or a contemporary steel sculpture that reads like a line drawing in space, metal offers a vivid contrast. Like many of the most valuable decorating details, it captures and sends back the light. It can be brushed, etched, perforated, or bathed in various solutions to produce finishes from pitted to sleek.

Offering distinction and durability, most metal reliably stands up to wear and may be used to great effect as an accent. Although perceived as hard, it is not without gentle connotations — consider the soft beauty of twining balusters wrought

Steel ascends to the stature of art in this Park Avenue duplex, which could be mistaken for a minimuseum of contemporary crafts. ▣ Bruce McLean designed the velvety fireplace (opposite), surrealistically scrawled with a cryptic X and a floating head. The cantilevered L-beam is a playful abstraction of a mantel, tilted just enough to energize the surrounding space but not enough to tip the vase. ▣ The same chameleonlike metal turns shiny and bright, now textured with saucy scribbles, on a wedge-shaped console table by Elizabeth Browning Jackson (above). Juxtaposed with a tilted cane and a dapper Borsalino, this piece looks ready to join the whimsical wicker umbrella stand in a vaudeville soft-shoe shuffle.

from iron, or bronze doorplates embossed with floral bouquets. It also evokes strong images. Yellow metals, such as brass and bronze, tend to connote tradition. (You can tell a lot about someone by whether or not he polishes his brass.) White metals like chrome and aluminum look machine-crafted, and are often associated with Modernism. Stainless-steel cabinets can look as nostalgic as a 1940s streamlined diner, or as futuristic as a space capsule. The Dorian Gray of materials, stainless steel defies time and doesn't age at all.

Metal adds a clean line and an incisive, modern edge to Eve Robinson's Manhattan apartment. ■ The designer's strategy was to take traditional elements and update them, like the sculptural sconces in the living room (above), crafted of coiled black iron. She invented a new system for hanging pictures, using clips that hook on a black iron rod; curtains hang from a slender rod of similar design. Stainless-steel sliding doors hide the entertainment center (opposite), and even the slipper chair is upholstered in a metallic stripe.

Expertly crafted metal simultaneously separates and opens up these spaces. ▓ Husband-and-wife architects Cathi and Steven House designed a double-sided fireplace (above) to divide living and dining areas in a contemporary California residence. Two tilted steel plates — dipped in a copper bath — collide with the more orthogonal stucco box, their conflicting geometries accenting a surface change from rough to matte. ▓ In a Manhattan penthouse (opposite), a filigreed brass railing from a Paris department store encloses the balcony, which overlooks a two-story atrium carved from a small narrow staircase by architect Nina Kardon Baron.

Metal may seem one of the most minimalist of materials, but its potential for expression is enormous. ■ A single slim iron rod bends and twists into each curlicue leg of a scalloped zinc table and stools (opposite), designed by Milanese architect Paola Navone for her kitchen in the Gorgonzola cheese warehouse she transformed into home. ■ A similar piecrust apron gives zinc shelves a primitive charm (above left); they hold spongeware, cobalt glass, and American mixing bowls, all in Navone's favorite shades of blue. ■ Strength and delicacy combine in a metal staircase and wrought-iron chandelier (above right), which is raised and lowered on a pulley. The huge oak beams, original to the space, are washed with lime. Navone applied concrete to the walls and ceilings, painting them with natural cobalt pigment that she let dry unevenly to show the touch of the hand.

THE painterly TOUCH

Color can be one of the most elusive and complex arenas of the designer's endeavor, and some will argue that a

room cannot really succeed until the mysteries of its pigments are solved.

Today's palettes are more alluring than ever, with a hundred shades of white alone, not to mention exotic tints to tempt the intrepid. Bored with sagacious neutrality? Turn up the volume in a room from cool green to burnt orange and the background comes forward and competes; pick out the trim in contrasting colors and the space goes graphic.

Muted, tremulous shades can be just as powerful in their own way. Designers often neutralize walls and ceilings to highlight the objects in a room. But the self-effacing color that defers to an Aubusson or an oriental carpet is not so shy as it might seem, for it relates by tone, undertone, or contrast to all the

It takes years to acquire this kind of patina — 300, at least, which is the approximate age of this enchanting house in the medieval French village of Hyères. Frédéric Méchiche was not about to tamper with it. ■ He merely preserved the time-washed surface, enhancing the rustic atmosphere with fine antiques and found objects, like the lanterns in the aqueous blue-green entrance hall (opposite), used to light the way to the guesthouse across the street. ■ In the dining area (above), all the furnishings are kept to the color of the crumbling plaster walls, which turns the background into foreground and brings out its mottled beauty. ■ Méchiche never even considered repainting the salon (overleaf), where he reupholstered the furniture by tacking on plain white sheeting.

furnishings and binds them into a whole. Subtle shades, mixed with a wider range of pigments than the two or three in a can of commercially mixed paint, seem to change color as the light hits from various angles as day draws to dusk.

The quickest face-lift for any tired room is a fresh coat of paint, which works just as well on the furniture as it does on the walls or ceiling. A dark formal armchair painted ivory relaxes and looks right at home in a cozy farmhouse. A plain pine chair acquires stature when the limbs are picked out in black and gold.

But color is not the end of the story. Texture and technique do so much to evoke a particular mood. Think of the hard, shiny veneer of Chinese red lacquer, the powdery whitewash on an old New England picket fence, or the flat, opaque surface by eighteenth-century milkpaint in cornflower blue.

Layer upon layer of thin glazes will create a luminous shimmer. Stippling, sponging, or the wavy lines of a brushed strié pattern add instant style to a room.

But adding age might be even more intriguing. Stir raw pigment into plaster and savor the Italianate aura it creates. Or, consider the possibility of paint *trouvé*; the worn, mottled surface of an old painted wall can be as evocative as an ancestral portrait.

More than mere painted rooms, these are rooms as paintings. Guests arriving at the 1595 Provençal farmhouse owned by French couturier Michel Klein and his associate Joel Fournier might think they had stepped into a Matisse. One rainy Sunday, Klein and Fournier got bored, bicycled to a local shop and came home with boxes of powdered pigments. Mixed into acrylic paint and thinned with water, the exuberant colors were ragged and brushed over the walls to luminous effect. ■ On-the-spot improvisation with a sponge produced the dappled blue wall in Fournier's bedroom (above). ■ Squiggles and dots in a striped hall (opposite) were done with pastel crayons.

Unexpected tones of chartreuse and celadon transform this once-ordinary plank floor into a work of art underfoot. Even the most material of elements becomes immaterial in Salle Werner Vaughn's hands, who designed and painted the compositions in her Houston cottage herself, mixing her own singular colors to contribute to the fanciful mood. This is paint as atmosphere, with the pattern on the floor plane rather than the walls. Even the window is blotted out with painters' dropcloths, hung from lengths of copper tubing with plumbing joints as the rings.

Paint can do almost anything carpet can. Here it adds a hint of color, without competing with the paintings propped against the wall in a room that serves Vaughn as both studio and gallery space. Diaphanous white gauze simply hemmed and folded over at the top of the windows filters the sunlight. The mood is ethereal, as light and airy as a soufflé. The empty frame poised against the wall introduces a note of mystery, and the sensation of walking — or is it floating? — on the whimsically painted floor only adds to the otherworldly atmosphere.

A SENSE OF
place

Anyone who has sat down to lunch on the sunswept deck of Nina Ramsey's Long Island beach cottage, waves lapping at their toes, knows this is the essence of summer at the shore. Simply put, her little house, painted pure white and open to sea and sky, has an evocative sense of place.

There was a time when climate and local materials shaped distinct regional building traditions by virtue of necessity. During the last century, however, machine-age metals and technological advances such as central heating and air-conditioning have increasingly liberated buildings from the need to respond to prevailing winds or a shifting sun.

Yet the characteristics identified with certain locales — a strong light, a dramatic landscape, a vital city skyline — continue to influence many designers today. They might capture a sense of place and time by using particular materials, historical features, architectural styles, or even a distinctive color palette. Whatever the approach, designs that respond to site, climate, and cultural conditions look rooted and appropriate. They belong, and become even more beautiful because house and place draw out each other's character.

THE
long island
SHORE

Only the lap of the waves and the cries of careening gulls break the silence. Alone on a rugged spit of land on Long Island bay, far from encroaching condominiums and the madding crowds of Manhattan, this elementary beach house is as simple as they come. Stark white, bare-boned, no curtains. "The house is just a shell," says Nina Ramsey, who designs linens for her own company, Archipelago, and shares this summer retreat with her film director husband, Greg. "All you see out of any window is water. You really feel like you're on a boat."

There are some interiors to which one should do very little. All the Ramseys did here was pour on white paint, then resist the temptation to clutter up the space. They kept the rooms deliberately underfurnished, pairing tag-sale rattan furniture with a basic white couch designed and built by Greg. Because each window frames the ocean, there is hardly a picture on the walls. The weather, in fact, is the Ramseys' decorator, and dictates the mood of the interior. The most prominent colors are the hues of the sea and sky outside, and those are constantly shifting. "We get the sunrise on one side of our bedroom and the sunset on the other," says Nina.

The house has no heat or insulation, so when the chill sets the couple shivering in November, they reluctantly board up the house until spring. Sometimes the rough sea sloshes through during a winter storm. But there's nothing precious for it to harm. It's as if the water has washed the house clean for their return in April, when the promise of long summer days beckons again.

This Long Island beach cottage is everything a summer house should be: bright, easy, airy. ▪ French doors in the living room open onto the deck (opposite), where the brilliant sun carves out patterns of light and shade. The 1950s pottery was collected at garage sales. ▪ A gently contoured Noguchi lamp (above) was the least obtrusive choice for a light fixture. ▪ Even the floral arrangements look as if they've just sprouted naturally in the living room (overleaf). Nina Ramsey designed the linen pillows with raffia fringe in the colors of beach glass and sand dunes so nothing inside would be brighter than the saturated blue of the sea. The house is a pristine backdrop to the miraculous ballet of light.

In the bedrooms, mosquito nets materialize the breeze. In true beach-cottage style, the underside of the roof was left exposed in the guest room and painted white to match the walls (above). Windsurfers are balanced on the crossbeams and it looks as if a guest could pick up a fishing pole and cast a line right out the window. Nina Ramsey made the witty lamp on the bedside table out of a half-scale dress form. ■ She also designed the initialed pillows in the master bedroom (opposite), where a continual flow of flotsam and jetsam gathered on the beach is arrayed on a windowsill.

new york

N E W   Y O R K

U NDERSTATEMENT IS NOT NORMALLY THE FIRST thing that comes to mind when people think of Manhattan. The Empire State Building, bagels and lox at the deli, the neon spangle of Broadway, kamikaze cabdrivers — plenty of images would probably take precedence.

But from the vantage point of the forty-third floor, the tumult and roar of the delirious city recede into remoteness in this apartment. Interior designer Benjamin Noriega-Ortiz arranged the high-rise aerie as an oasis of calm for fashion designer Steve Fabrikant and his family. "They wanted a subdued, simple backdrop for the objects they collect," says Noriega-Ortiz. But like the proverbial little black dress, which Fabrikant styles with a distinctive gold button accentuating just the right body curve or slice of skin, the simplicity is deceptive. The decoration is here, it is just supremely subtle.

It starts with the core of the apartment itself. The layout was good, but the building's typical postwar construction looked like cardboard. Working closely with Fabrikant, who has studied architecture, Noriega-Ortiz thickened the flimsy interior walls to twelve inches from the original five, replaced puny doors with seven-foot-wide portals, and chose one color — white with a light pink cast — for walls and ceilings. Add one huge gilt mirror, unusual decorative objects, and pared-down furniture, and nothing else is needed to make a bland box look sublimely vast and vaporous. The apartment reflects the sophistication of a city that has always been the final repository for fine antiques, ambitious people, and inspiring design.

Reflecting the study (opposite), the eighteenth-century French Provençal mirror in the living room was too large for the elevator and had to be hoisted up forty-three floors and over the balcony. ■ An antique shaving cabinet (above) holds keys. ■ Nickel-plated studs adorn a movable partition dividing study and living room (overleaf). Noriega-Ortiz built the low wall behind the two easy chairs so those entering the room would at first see no furniture, only the view beyond. Noriega-Ortiz, who favors effortlessly elegant fabrics with just enough sheen to catch the light, fought for the iridescent silk damask on the chaise. The clients had requested solid-colored materials — but now they love it.

High-heeled furniture: A 1950s chair upholstered in black silk tailored with nickel studs slinks up to the Biedermeier dining table (above left). ▪ Fabrikant found the 1940s Robsjohn-Gibbings desk shaped like an ironing board (above right), now poised in the study. The maple floorboards were rubbed with a bit of pink-tinged white paint to unify the sculptural shell of the apartment; walls and ceiling are painted the same hue. All the windows are covered with linen gauze, attached to the ceiling to show more of the fabric and soften the architecture. ▪ In the bedroom (opposite) motorized blinds shut out dawn's early light. Creamy calfskin drapes a table and upholsters the base of the kingsize bed. The headboard is slipcovered in white plissé and the spread is a snowy matelassé.

NEW
england

GEORGE WASHINGTON NEVER SLEPT HERE, BUT HE did in fact confer with the Marquis de Lafayette in this 1770 Connecticut house, originally built as a tavern. More than two centuries later, its classic features — peaked roof with a discreetly ornamented cornice, pedimented doorway, twelve-over-twelve double-hung window sash, thick stone walls — attest to the enduring appeal of New England's traditional colonial architecture.

The plain but handsome interior woodwork suited the taste of fashion designer Bill Blass, the current owner. Blass is a man who lives simply, among beautiful things. Respecting its inherent modesty, he did not smother the austere house with chintz-covered sofas and armchairs. He scraped off twenty layers of paint that masked the mellow wood in the dining room. There are no elaborate draperies at the deep-set windows because Blass is opposed on principle to any kind of curtains. "I hate all that fabric," he complains. "I tend to like rooms that are plain and not colorful. Maybe it's because I'm in the fashion business and I tire of all that."

When he first moved into the house, Blass bought American primitive furniture, but then realized he coudn't live with only that. Yet the pieces he added, including Scottish benches and a two-tiered marble-topped table from France, seem to have a natural affinity with the strong lines of the early American pieces. "I tend to pick the unusual, and I like to mix things," says the designer, who appreciates good fit and proportion, and found both in this house.

This flagstone terrace (opposite) is where Bill Blass goes to arrange peonies from his gardens. ■ Like many houses in New England, his late eighteenth-century country retreat in rural Connecticut (above) was built of granite from a local quarry. The solid masonry retains heat in winter and keeps the interior refreshingly cool in summer. The classical cornice, with modillions and corner returns, is typical of Georgian-period buildings and reflects the influence of English taste on colonial builders. The attic window is a Greek Revival element, perhaps added some years after the house was built.

The corner cupboard in the former tavern's private dining room (above) was made by Paul Revere's carpenter, and may have come from Revere's own New England house. The Palladian design, incorporating an arch, central keystone, and fluted pilasters on the sides, is found in many Connecticut houses of the period, but the cabriole leglike detail is unusual. ■ The deep window openings dictated by the thick stone walls in the dining room (opposite), as well as throughout the house, are splayed to let in more light. ■ Primitive American sideboards contrast neatly with silver candelabras at the dining room windows (overleaf). The cupboard over the mantel was to hold gun-powder and to keep it dry. A previous owner removed the beaded boards that originally encased the beams to reveal their hand-hewn surfaces.

THE DEEP
south

IN FLORIDA, IT'S NOT THE HEAT, IT'S THE HUMIDITY, so for a vacation retreat on the Atlantic coast, Hugh Newell Jacobsen dipped into tropical architectural traditions to create a house that pays homage to water and coaxes breezes out of thick air. Located in the new town of Windsor, a planned community built from the ground up, this house had to conform to strict codes. These are intended to respect local building custom by restricting the height, materials, and siting of all structures to keep them in context with each other and the region at large. Jacobsen, a Washington, D.C. architect, has built far and wide, and is renowned for adapting local vernaculars into designs that are nonetheless unique. Here, he somehow manages to follow the rules exactly and yet wind up with a house that looks like nothing else in town.

Jacobsen's signature technique is to distill the outside of his structures to the most basic regional features, then shed all parochial references inside in favor of pure white rooms. In this house, he incorporates elements traditionally used in Florida: stucco-covered cinderblock, which holds up to humidity; drop siding (the boards are flush); pine shingles; and louvered shutters. "These are natural ventilators," says Jacobsen, "allowing the passage of air while filtering the sun." Then he puts these components together in an unconventional way, elongating proportions to create unusually generous spaces.

The two-and-a-half story living room is not only elegant, but also practical. "Hot air rises, so I stretched the height," says the architect. A ceiling fan encourages any

Andres Duany and Elizabeth Plater-Zyberk, the same design team that created the model Panhandle town of Seaside, also developed guidelines for Windsor. Jacobsen was required to build up to the lot lines of this corner site but leave 35 percent of it open to the sky. ■ Between the summer pavilion and the main house (opposite), he created a walled courtyard for complete privacy, rimmed with thirty-two grapefruit trees as a reminder of the grove that once grew on the property. ■ Traditional wooden louvers that hinge on top, known as Bermuda shutters, enclose the streetside balcony (above). "It's the perfect place to hang the laundry," says the architect.

breeze that wafts in through tall multipaned windows. Actually pocket doors, these slide back into the wall. Each elongated window is topped by a smaller nine-pane square. "That's a very neoclassical detail — the square window over a long one," says Jacobsen. "Palladio did it."

The living room was designed to look down the length of the property to a symmetrically massed pavilion that repeats the same forms. Then, in a dramatic gesture, the architect ran a 25-by-47-foot pool from the wall of one structure right up to the other. It is literally possible to slide open a living room window, dive out, and swim to the pavilion.

"Water is one of the oldest architectural tools we have, and the closer you can get it to the house, the more exciting it is," says Jacobsen. As the sun moves past the meridian, the ceilings sparkle with reflections from the pool. Quivers of light bounce off the walls. In the sultry heat of a Floridian August, a quick dip promises instant refreshment. In this house, the residents can leave the air-conditioning off.

In the dining room (above) the table is a simple slab of travertine covered with a linen cloth. ■ Jacobsen designed the pavilion (opposite) as a folly that could eventually function as a guest house with the addition of a bathroom and bedroom on the second floor. For now, the two-story room is open to the breeze, with no glass or screens. The interior is clad with the same drop siding as the exterior to blur the boundaries between indoors and out. The pool laps up to the doorsill. "Everybody always worries that it will flood over," says the architect. "But how many pools overflow?"

Around the mantel (left) an eighteenth-century English paneling design was abstracted to create an all-white storage wall that hides the television, stereo, and woodbox. "I use white because it has the presence of all colors in it," says Jacobsen. "It's always changing, and it makes people look good." ■ Couches gathered around a steel coffee table are in the same cool tones (below).

In the two-and-one-half-story living room (opposite) and throughout the house, the floor is precast concrete tinted snow white; imprints of coral stone recall the *coquina* stone quarried by Florida's Spanish colonial settlers. "You'd never know it was concrete, because the forms never repeat," says Jacobsen. "It should be sealed twice a year to keep out mildew."

For the master bedroom (above), the architect designed a four-poster bed made of steel with a faux-bronze finish. The mattress sits 30 inches high, taller than normal, because he likes that exaggerated proportion. The slim horizontal slot in the ceiling handles the air-conditioning. Floor-to-ceiling windows intentionally make the space look larger. ■ A sunken tub was chosen for the bathroom (opposite) for the same reason. Indoor shutters close off the window facing the courtyard for privacy.

THE AMERICAN heartland

where, on a summer evening, people sit on their front porch with a pitcher of lemonade and neighbors passing by step up for a chat. Children on bicycles weave down the street trailed by expectant terriers, and on Saturday morning lawnmowers whir like insects.

This rambling gray-shingled 1890s Victorian in Illinois is just such a house in just such a town. It typifies the new suburban residences of the late 1800s, when improved transportation made it possible for families to move outside cities to roomy houses with spacious yards and porches that served as outdoor rooms. "This style of house is uniquely American," says New York designer Mark Hampton, who decorated the interiors for his sister. "It has a great light, airy quality and none of that dark heaviness usually associated with the nineteenth century."

Hampton's sister has lived in the house for twenty-five years, and furnishing it has been a family affair, taking place over time. "Fortunately my sister and I have the same taste; I like a lot of pattern, and so does she," says Hampton. Wallpaper would have enlivened the rooms originally, and still does today. "The windows are so complicated that you can't have complicated curtains, so wallpaper carries a big decorative load," he adds. Victorian rose-back chairs, inherited from their parents, look perfect next to ample easy chairs upholstered in chintz. The pileup of pattern seems to suit the idiosyncratic architecture, punctuated with bowed windows and odd corners. Hampton and his sister wanted the house to feel light and bright, yet still romantic and old-fashioned and cozy. They succeeded. This looks like a house that has been lived in and loved.

This gracious Victorian is on a quiet street lined with houses of similar vintage in a part of town that remains remarkably unchanged since the 1890s. ■ An ample front porch (opposite) was a staple of the midwestern streetscape during the late nineteenth century, a health-conscious era when the benefits of fresh air were highly touted. ■ The fanciful jigsawn brackets with drop pendants (above) could be ordered inexpensively from catalogues. And what could be more American than a white picket fence and a flag flying at the entrance?

Original to the house, the living room fireplace (above) displays a neo-Colonial Revival design; such features were popular in the late Victorian era, when builders began to borrow from America's early architecture. ■ The voluptuous, heart-shaped swoon of a sofa (right) is the sort of shape Mark Hampton adores. In the hall beyond, he used darker, stronger colors as a counterpoint to the lighter living room. The block-print wallpaper "furnishes" the space, too small for real furniture of its own.

Blue-and-white Staffordshire lines the shelves and every available surface in the pantry (above); some pieces were handed down from Hampton's mother and grandmother. The pantry cabinets are all original to the 1890s house. ■ Roses in the pattern of the dining room wallpaper (opposite) are even more lush than the roses from the garden. The chandelier is a reproduction of a gas fixture from the Victorian era. Two sets — six each — of almost identical William IV chairs were found in London. French doors open up the room to a side porch.

DOWNTOWN
chicago

THERE ARE THOSE APARTMENTS THAT LIVE IN AND for their view. They are the 747s of real estate, offering the sun, moon, stars, and other constellations of high-flying penthouses as neighbors in the sky. This corner apartment in one of the famed landmark twin towers designed in 1951 by Mies van der Rohe on Chicago's Lake Shore Drive looks out on Lake Michigan and the downtown skyline. When the owners acquired the apartment directly above theirs, architects Ronald Krueck and Mark Sexton were commissioned to combine the two spaces into one duplex.

Their urbane composition of machine-age materials was cribbed from the city outside. Rolled stainless steel, more typically used on subway cars and buses, faces kitchen cabinets. High-gloss car paint gives a storage wall in the master bedroom a luminous sheen. A movable slice of sandblasted glass closes off the study. Floors, except in the carpeted bedrooms, are paved with glass-chip terrazzo — virtually maintenance-free.

Inserting the stairs posed the greatest challenge. "Suddenly we were dealing with vertical space in a horizontal Mies apartment, where the compression between the floor and ceiling planes projected you out into the view," says Sexton. To reinforce that dynamic, they aimed the stairs straight at the lake. Guests enter above, where the living room is situated, then walk down the stairs "and off the edge of the earth," to the kitchen and dining area.

This apartment proudly proclaims its modernity at every turn. When Mies designed these towers, the city held great promise. Krueck and Sexton have recaptured that sense of optimism and romance.

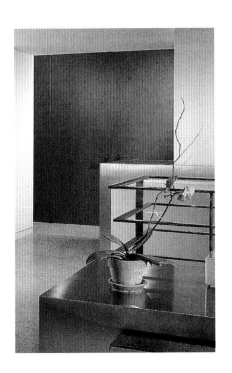

In the living room (opposite), furniture is kept low and horizontal to defer to the view of downtown Chicago. Chunky easy chairs upholstered in midnight-blue mohair reflect the colors of the nighttime sky. ■ No moldings or superfluous surface decoration interferes with the design: Two panels open out of a teak wall (above) to form the front door. ■ A guest entering the apartment on the top floor is immediately catapulted into the view (overleaf). Long, lean built-in couches against the staircase wall keep the space uncluttered. "We tried to put in curves, but it didn't work," says architect Ronald Krueck. "Everything ended up rectilinear."

Throughout the apartment, surfaces are reflective without being actual mirrors, creating an effect much like light rippling on water. ■ In a characteristically inventive use of industrial materials, the dining table (opposite) is made of three different textures of glass laminated together. ■ The staircase (above) is a stream-lined Busby Berkeley stage set of prismatic steel-plate, nuts, and bolts, all floating above an ebony landing. A trio of lightboxes on the partition separating the dining area from the family room casts a soft glow, ideal for an intimate supper.

THE
great lakes

THE FLAT, WINDSWEPT COUNTRYSIDE OF THE MIDWEST inspired one of America's greatest architectural legacies, Frank Lloyd Wright's Prairie house. With their horizontal lines, low-pitched roofs with deep overhanging eaves, and broad terraces, these houses seem to embrace the landscape, while organic materials such as wood and sun-warmed stone deftly tie them to the earth.

When architect Stephen Byrns was asked to design a weekend home on the shore of Lake Michigan for a couple with four grown children and an expanding assortment of grandchildren, he remembered that heritage. Instead of the "modern" house the clients thought they wanted, Byrns proposed one inspired by Wright's early-twentieth-century Prairie houses across the Michigan border in nearby Oak Park, Illinois.

His design would also draw on the closely allied Arts and Crafts movement, founded in late-nineteenth century England by William Morris and John Ruskin, who advocated a revival of the handcraftsmanship lost to an industrial age. Wright was influenced by their philosophy and helped found the Chicago Arts and Crafts Society in 1897.

"Wright's Prairie houses were a hinge point between traditional and modern architecture," says Byrns. "They still had that old richness of detail, but brought a new freedom in plan." Here, following Wright's example, space flows freely through the house with the generosity of the prairie, instead of being confined by small, boxy rooms. Large expanses of glass help open the interior to the outdoors, and a band of transom windows at

Respectful of material and craftsmanship, Stephen Byrns acknowledges a debt both to the Arts and Crafts movement and the low-slung Prairie houses of Frank Lloyd Wright. ■ To reinforce the horizontal massing of this Michigan house, every third course of shingles is doubled to create a shadow line across the facade (opposite). The arched wishbone bracket above the living room window is a modern version of a traditional Arts and Crafts detail from the turn of the century. ■ Made of willow and aspen boughs, the rocker and table on the screened porch (above) were designed by Michigan craftsman Clifton Monteith.

both stories echoes the dominant horizontality of the landscape. Inside, that band is extended around the perimeter of each room and accentuated in various ways: with wallpaper; a gridded frieze of bird's-eye maple; grilles of slender wood spindles.

In an era of sheetrock walls and other construction shortcuts, Byrns has managed to maintain a remarkable level of workmanship. Following the lead of Morris and Ruskin, he has shaped a total aesthetic from floor to ceiling.

The flattened moldings and decorative wood panels characteristic of the Arts and Craft style are meticulously recreated. Built-in furniture represents a simpler version of the glorious oak pieces created by Wright for his Prairie houses. A wealth of detailing, worked in quarter-sawn white oak, makes this large residence — there are six bedrooms and four and a half baths — feel surprisingly intimate.

Outside, the house is clad in cedar shingles, which Byrns felt were appropriate to the location on the sand dunes just 300 feet from the lake. A manicured lawn would have looked too suburban; instead, the architect sited this grand old-fashioned family house to save every tree possible, then surrounded it with azaleas, lilacs, laurel, and beach grasses to reinforce the dunes.

Over the library fireplace, two different marbles — Red Verona and Rouge Antique — pick up the color and pattern of the bird's-eye maple frieze (above). Family members collected the stones on the beach. ■ Byrns designed built-in banquettes under the bay window (opposite) in the spirit of Frank Lloyd Wright, who integrated furniture and structure into a seamless, organic whole. He also adopted the multipaned windows characteristic of traditional Arts andCrafts cottages, combining them with larger expanses of glass to open up the house.

Earth tones are characteristic of the Arts and Crafts aesthetic. ■ The wallpaper in the dining room (left) is in the style of the English artist William Morris; covering the ceiling as well as the walls, it produces a warm, encompassing effect. A double-wide border continues the horizontal band established by the wood truss and multipaned window transoms. ■ The bay window (above) captures a long view up the shoreline.

THE california
COAST

that anyone sitting with a glass of Chardonnay on the terrace can hear the foam of a spent wave sizzle into the sand. The alluring curve of the California coastline — a rugged cliff of rock and scrub — dissolves in the distance into the amethyst blur of the Santa Ynez Mountains.

That boundless view straight to the shimmering, sunstruck horizon line where ocean meets sky is this house's reason for being. Here, architecture is not the point. Not that whoever built this redwood contemporary back in the 1970s didn't try. The double-height living room was a nice touch — though unfortunately paneled in redwood as well. "Imagine living in a cedar closet," deadpans television writer Susan Harris, who owns the house with her husband and partner, producer Paul Witt.

Designers Joseph Lembo and Laura Bohn came to the rescue. They pickled the garish paneling to a soft gray, demolished extraneous walls, corrected the awkward pitch of the roof, and generally reproportioned the house to accommodate traffic patterns and take better advantage of the site. An exterior wall of the master bedroom was moved forward about three feet to steal space for a tight master bath. A solid balcony railing, which blocked the view of the waves for anyone lying in bed, was replaced with thin metal railings, now entwined with wisteria.

Lembo and Bohn specialize in the juxtaposition of the rustic and the refined. Harris and Witt share that sensibility, with an equally sophisticated eye. The bedroom walls are coated with matte-finish plaster tinted sea green, with bits of the raw pigment showing through. In the living room, primitive

Flushed rose with the sunset, fossilized stone from Mexico paves a terrace facing the Pacific (opposite); the Cinemascope view was the single most important influence on this California house remodeled by Joseph Lembo and Laura Bohn. Teak chairs surround a simple table made of poured concrete, topped with a market umbrella from Italy. ■ In the living room, candlesticks for every occasion congregate on a tabletop in front of a diptych by Helen Frankenthaler (above).

urns mingle with impeccably tailored silk cotton upholstery and sleek leather chairs. "They love things that are old, rusted, chipped, and cracked," says Bohn. "Anything with a patina to it, they appreciate. We do, too."

The color scheme takes its cues from the chromatics of the California coastline. "This house is so connected to the water," declares Lembo. "The living room is all watery blue and lavender, very cool and ethereal, like the blue light reflected from the sea." Inside, the palette goes from taupe to Technicolor, with stops at driftwood and sage green.

The redwood exterior has been painted a weathered gray to blend in with the vegetation. Fragrant lemon trees shade the path through wall-to-wall flowers up to the front door. Inside, the first thing one feels is the breeze blowing through the house. "Now the interior flows beautifully to the ocean," says Witt. "You're immediately transported," adds Lembo. "It's paradise."

A relief map of France, which the owners found at a Paris flea market, hangs in the dining area (above). The beautifully proportioned Chippendale chair is one of a pair the designers bleached for a lighter, more casual look. The mother-of-pearl buttons on the chartreuse slipcover came out of Bohn's button box; she has a collection of more than 20,000. ■ Silk cotton in underwater colors — mauve, purple, and blue — upholsters the custom-made furniture in the two-story living room (opposite). The crusted tin pediment above the fireplace once crowned a building in New York City. Eroded and scrolled, the piece embodies the room's blend of rusticity and elegance in one sophisticated gesture.

The master bedroom looks straight out to the ocean (left). Lacquered in a pale ice blue, the paneled wall behind the bed is a typical Lembo/Bohn detail. In order to give the illusion of more space, it doesn't touch the ceiling. ■ The headboard is slipcovered in Fortuny cotton and a Cy Twombley painting hangs over the sandstone fireplace surround. ■ Necklaces spill from an antique mahogany box on a dressing table in the master bath (above).

THE southwest

the sky and drains the color from the mountains that corrugate the landscape around Scottsdale, Arizona. Just beyond the art galleries and manicured golf courses is the fatal beauty of the Sonora Desert where the saguaro cactus stands sentinel. Dangerous to cross in the 115-degree heat of July, the aloof terrain is a blur of bloom after the rains.

In the heart of town, however, the desert has been domesticated, with only the stray yucca in decorator Nancy Kitchell's courtyard as a reminder of the primitive landscape nearby. Her new house is deliberately not adobe. Yet there are certain echoes of the vernacular in the one-story residence built of cement block and stucco: the thickness of the battered exterior walls, splayed at the bottom to support the weight of the heavy masonry, as well as a particular attitude toward light. For years, Southwesterners have instinctively followed a passive solar approach, emphasizing the northern, southern, and eastern exposures, and protecting the interior of a structure from the western glare. There are no windows on the west facade at all.

Kitchell's house is basically a rectangular box, as elemental in shape as the spheres and squares of the old baseballs and dice that she collects. One large room, long enough for two fireplaces on the same wall, functions as living, dining, and entertainment area. Simple concrete pavers cover the floor. White paint unifies the walls.

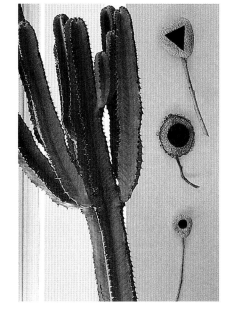

Sidestepping the adobe stereotype, Nancy Kitchell built her Arizona house with cement block and stucco (opposite), painted the gray of an ironwood tree. More than five inches thick, the brushed aluminum front door designed by local artist Jim O'Hara feels like the entrance to a vault. ■ Another regional artist, Michael Marlowe, painted geometric forms on sunflower seedpods, mounted next to a euphorbia cactus (above). ■ Earth tones bring a sense of calm and security to the living area (overleaf). "It draws you in, like the desert," says Kitchell of the multipurpose space. The silver sphere in the foreground is said to ward off witches.

The furnishings are eclectic. That main room holds a rustic Mexican table, with roots connected to this region, but it is joined by 1950s sling-back leather chairs, a Japanese tansu chest, Louis XV-style bergères, and an Egyptian-Revival Thebes chair.

The local color comes from works by regional artists, interspersed with overscaled potted cacti, which endow the ensemble with a Southwestern accent. "It's an odd mix, but it seems to fascinate people," says Kitchell. "It's casual enough so they can really be comfortable, and interesting enough that they want to come back."

A wall-to-wall clerestory window under the ceiling in the dining area (above) lets in a dazzling streak of light. The tall cabinet may have come out of an old general store. ■ There's no kitsch in Kitchell's version of Southwestern style, just strong graphic elements enhanced by a spiraling ceramic piece made by Jun Kaneko mounted over the simple cement fireplace (opposite). An African game board sits on the granite table, and an African oar leans against the wall.

The second fireplace on the long wall anchors the entertainment area (opposite), where Kitchell can curl up on one of a pair of chaises and listen to her son play the bass or the guitar. The nineteenth-century altar table under the window came from the Philippines. ■ Kitchell designed the overscaled, overstuffed sleigh bed (above) when she was pregnant. A paper dress pattern from Haiti hangs over it. Against the wall is Kitchell's version of an old gypsy cabinet belonging to a friend; Kitchell loved the piece so much she had it copied. A teak deck chair in the foreground and a black-and-gold painted Thebes chair pulled up to the glass desktop bring a few more cultures to the intriguing mix.

directory
OF DESIGNERS AND ARCHITECTS

GAE AULENTI
Milan, Italy

CHRISTIAN BADIN
Paris, France

NINA KARDON BARON
Brookline, Massachusetts

BARBARA BARRY
Barbara Barry Incorporated
Los Angeles, California

LAURA BOHN AND
    JOSEPH LEMBO
Lembo Bohn Design Associates
New York, New York

NANCY BRAITHWAITE
Nancy Braithwaite Interiors, Inc.
Atlanta, Georgia

STEPHEN F. BYRNS
Byrns, Kendall and Schieferdecker
    Architects
New York, New York

FU-TUNG CHENG
Cheng Design and Construction, Inc.
Berkeley, California

VINCENT DANÉ
Melissa Wyndham & Vincent Dané Ltd.
London, England

TOM FOX AND JOE NAHEM
Fox-Nahem Design
New York, New York

MARK HAMPTON
Mark Hampton, Inc.
New York, New York

MARIETTE HIMES GOMEZ
Gomez Associates
New York, New York

JACQUES GRANGE
Paris, France

ANN HOLDEN AND
    ANN DUPUY
Holdon & Dupuy
New Orleans, Louisiana

ALBERT HADLEY
Parish-Hadley Associates, Inc.
New York, New York

VICTORIA HAGAN
Victoria Hagan Interiors
New York, New York

WILLIAM HODGINS
William Hodgins, Inc.
Boston, Massachusetts

CATHI AND STEVEN HOUSE
House + House
San Francisco, California

HAL MARTIN JACOBS
Hal Martin Jacobs & Associates
New York, New York

HUGH NEWELL JACOBSEN
Hugh Newell Jacobsen Architects
Washington, DC

CHRISTIAN LIAIGRE
Liaigre Design Co.
Paris, France
(in the U.S. through Holly Hunt Ltd.,
    New York, New York)

NANCY KITCHELL
Kitchell Interior Design Associates
Scottsdale, Arizona

RONALD KRUECK AND
    MARK SEXTON
Krueck & Sexton Architects
Chicago, Illinois

RANDOLPH MARTZ
Randolph Martz Architect
Charleston, South Carolina

FRÉDÉRIC MÉCHICHE
Gallery Frédéric Méchiche
Paris, France

NANCY MULLAN
Kitchens, Inc.
New York, New York

PAOLA NAVONE
Milan, Italy

BENJAMIN NORIEGA-ORTIZ
New York, New York

SANDRA NUNNERLY
Sandra Nunnerly, Inc.
New York, New York

KATHRYN OGAWA
    AND GILLES DEPARDON
Ogawa/Depardon
New York, New York

EVE ROBINSON
Eve Robinson Associates, Inc.
New York, New York

JOHN SALADINO
John F. Saladino, Inc.
New York, New York

SERGIO AND MONIQUE
    SAVARESE
Dialogica
New York, New York

PAUL SISKIN
Siskin Valls, Inc.
New York, New York

CHARLES SPADA
Charles Spada Interiors
Boston, Massachusetts

MICHAEL STANLEY
Michael Stanley Design
Thompson, Connecticut

SALLE WERNER VAUGHN
Harmonium
Houston, Texas

BUNNY WILLIAMS
Bunny Williams, Inc.
New York, New York

VICENTE WOLF
Vicente Wolf Associates
New York, New York

ACKNOWLEDGMENTS

House Beautiful would like to thank homeowners Virginia and Michael White,
Susie and Edward Elliott Elson, Rachel and Rolf Blank, Shirlee and David Levin, Sharon and
Jeffrey Casdin, Marc Blondeau, Sebastien Blondeau, Dolph Leuthold, Thomas K. Woodard,
Blanche Greenstein, Janet Kardon, and Pierre and Georgette Depardon.

The room on page 1 was designed by Mariette Himes Gomez; page 5, Bunny Williams;
page 6, Frédéric Méchiche; page 218, Barbara Barry; page 221, Nancy Mullan;
page 222, Michael Stanley; page 224, Robert Hill.

The photographs on pages 66–69 and 221 were taken at the
Kips Bay Boys and Girls Club Show House, New York, New York

photography

CREDITS

1	Thibault Jeanson
2	Catherine Leuthold
6–7	Jacques Dirand
20–27	Dominique Vorillon
28–33	William Waldron
34–39	Antoine Bootz
40–45	Dominique Vorillon
46–53	Peter Estersohn
54–59	Thibault Jeanson
60–65	Jacques Dirand
66–69	Thibault Jeanson
70–75	Peter Estersohn
76–81	Thibault Jeanson
82–89	Jacques Dirand
90–91	Thibault Jeanson
92–93	Antoine Bootz
94–95	Elizabeth Zeschin
96–97	David Glomb
98–99	Richard Felber
100–101	Catherine Leuthold
102–103	Jacques Dirand
104	Jack Winston
106–107	Lizzie Himmel
108–109	William Waldron
110–114	Antoine Bootz
115	Dominique Vorillon
116–117	Antoine Bootz
118–119	Lizzie Himmel
120–121	Michael Dunne
122–123	Peter Margonelli
124	William Waldron (left) Peter Margonelli (right)
125	Fran Brennan
126–127	Jacques Dirand
128–129	Thibault Jeanson
130	William Waldron
131	Michael Skott
132–133	Langdon Clay
134–135	Antoine Bootz
136–137	Alan Weintraub
138	Alex McClean
139	William Waldron
140	Jacques Dirand
141	Langdon Clay (left) Jacques Dirand (right)
142–143	Jacques Dirand
144–145	Peter Margonelli
146	Christopher Irion
147	Jacques Dirand
148–149	Oberto Gili
150–153	Jacques Dirand
154–155	Oberto Gili
156–157	Fran Brennan
158–165	Lizzie Himmel
166–171	Peter Margonelli
172–177	Antoine Bootz
178–185	Robert Lautman
186–191	Antoine Bootz
192–197	Paul Warchol
198–203	Langdon Clay
204–209	Dominique Vorillon
210–217	Jacques Dirand
218	Dominique Vorillon
224	Thibault Jeanson

index